T0012934

# LOW-SODIUM COOKING
## Made Easy

Eat Well and
Maintain Health
Naturally with
Less Salt

DICK LOGUE

NEW SHOE PRESS

Inspiring | Educating | Creating | Entertaining

Brimming with creative inspiration, how-to projects, and useful information to enrich your everyday life, quarto.com is a favorite destination for those pursuing their interests and passions.

© 2023 Quarto Publishing Group USA Inc.

First Published in 2023 by New Shoe Press, an imprint of The Quarto Group, 100 Cummings Center, Suite 265-D, Beverly, MA 01915, USA.
T (978) 282-9590 F (978) 283-2742 Quarto.com

All rights reserved. No part of this book may be reproduced in any form without written permission of the copyright owners. All images in this book have been reproduced with the knowledge and prior consent of the artists concerned, and no responsibility is accepted by producer, publisher, or printer for any infringement of copyright or otherwise, arising from the contents of this publication. Every effort has been made to ensure that credits accurately comply with information supplied. We apologize for any inaccuracies that may have occurred and will resolve inaccurate or missing information in a subsequent reprinting of the book.

New Shoe Press titles are also available at discount for retail, wholesale, promotional, and bulk purchase. For details, contact the Special Sales Manager by email at specialsales@quarto.com or by mail at The Quarto Group, Attn: Special Sales Manager, 100 Cummings Center, Suite 265-D, Beverly, MA 01915, USA.

ISBN: 978-0-7603-8019-2
eISBN: 978-0-7603-8020-8

Library of Congress Cataloging-in-Publication Data available.

The content in this book was previously published in *500 Low Sodium Recipes* (Fair Winds Press 2007) by Dick Logue.

Photography: Shutterstock

The information in this book is for educational purposes only. It is not intended to replace the advice of a physician or medical practitioner. Please see your health-care provider before beginning any new health program.

# Contents

# All About Low Sodium

*The ingredients you use have a significant effect on the amount of sodium in recipes. In many cases you'll have to make a choice about ingredients that can make the difference between a recipe that is low in sodium and one that isn't. This chapter will help you understand what low sodium ingredients are, where to find them, and how to determine whether ingredients are indeed low sodium (since some of these nutrition labels can be somewhat misleading).*

Low sodium ingredients are one way of reducing the amount of sodium in a recipe. (Another way is leaving out things that are high in sodium, like salt.)

Low sodium ingredients can take several forms. The simplest case involves being choosy about what ingredients you buy. Many items now are available in "no-salt-added" versions. This includes things like canned vegetables and beans, broths and bouillon, and spice blends.

In other cases you may be able to find a slightly different product that is meant as a replacement for high sodium ones. There are sodium-free versions of items such as baking powder and baking soda that traditionally contain a lot of sodium.

The last category of low sodium ingredients is those you make yourself. Some items are just impossible to find in a low sodium version or are much more expensive. In those cases you may want to consider making your own low sodium version. I've included recipes for some of these in Chapter 3: Basic Ingredients.

## What about Salt Substitutes?

A number of salt substitutes are available on the market. In many cases, these products replace the sodium chloride with potassium chloride. This has several potential drawbacks. Some medical conditions may require you to limit potassium as well as sodium, so these products would not be acceptable. Also, potassium chloride tends to have a metallic aftertaste that many people object to. Some of the newer products have other ingredients in addition to the potassium chloride, so the aftertaste is less noticeable.

I've personally never used salt substitutes. In the first place I wasn't fond of the flavor. I also thought that they might interfere with the process of getting used to the taste of food without salt. I don't really know if it's true or not, but it seemed to me that in order to lose the desire for salty flavor, you should give up everything that is salty tasting, even things such as salt substitutes that do not contain sodium. You'll need to decide whether these products are right for you, with the help of your medical professional.

## Where Do I Find Low Sodium Ingredients?

The first place to look for low sodium ingredients is in your local grocery stores. I can't tell you what may be available at your local market, wherever in the world you may be, but I find a number of low sodium ingredients locally. I shop at several of the large supermarket chains, a couple of discount clubs, and one local store. I buy many of the items I use at one of these places. They all carry different things, but between them I find quite a few low sodium items. I also stop by my local health food store occasionally. Since many of the manufacturers involved in organic products also tend to make salt-free ones, you'll find health food stores to be a good source, especially for spices and canned products. Any of these stores, either the grocery or health food ones, carry what they think will sell, and the store manager has some discretion in choosing those items. So letting your store manager know that you want low sodium items stocked may help. I've seen cases where a manager will order something new for you and others where they don't, because they feel the space could be used for something that more people want. It never hurts to ask.

Another great source of low sodium foods is stores that specialize in organic and gourmet foods like Whole Foods and Trader Joe's. If you live near one of these, or some similar store, you should definitely check them out. You can get a list of locations from their websites.

I'm going to mention a couple of online sources because they carry a large variety of low sodium items. First is Healthy Heart Market at www.healthyheartmarket.com. They specialize in low sodium items and carry some things that you probably didn't even know came in low sodium versions. Pete Eiden, who founded Healthy Heart Market, is a congestive heart failure patient who saw a need to provide low sodium products for people like him who needed to maintain a low sodium lifestyle. He is a great guy, and actually got me started sharing this information when he published one of my recipes in his newsletter. You can read his medical story on his website. Healthy Heart Market ships to the United States or Canada.

The second online source that I use often is Salt Watcher at www.saltwatcher.com. Gayle Michler, the founder, is a registered nurse who saw a need for easy access to low sodium products. She also carries a large variety of all low sodium items, including some deli items and cheeses, as well as other hard-to-find items. At this time Salt Watcher only ships to the United States, but you might want to check the site to see if that has changed since I wrote this.

The service at both of these sites is great, the prices and shipping costs are reasonable, and the selection is extensive. Besides that, it makes good sense to patronize those places that are striving to make a living providing the products that we all need and often find difficult to locate. It's a win for both sides.

## The Importance of Reading Labels

If you haven't already done this, I would suggest that one of the most useful things you can do is to take an hour or two and spend them just wandering up and down the aisles of your local supermarket, picking up things you would normally use and reading the labels. Take a pad of paper and pen and take notes, so you can remember what low sodium items you found. Not only will this get you started in thinking about how much sodium is in certain foods, but also if you check different brands or types of the same food, you'll often find that one has a lot less sodium than the others.

Some things are almost always high in sodium.

### Pay Special Attention to These Items

- canned vegetables
- prepared foods like canned soup and chili
- packaged mixes
- frozen meals and entrees
- cured meats like ham and bacon
- sauces and salad dressings

You may find low sodium versions of some of those if you look. Our local stores here in southern Maryland, for instance, all carry no-salt-added canned tomatoes, stewed tomatoes, tomato sauce, and tomato paste. low sodium versions of other items like chili and soups are harder to find. As always, read the labels carefully.

The following are the rules for sodium labeling in the United States established by the Food and Drug Administration.

| FDA RULES FOR SODIUM LABELING IN THE UNITED STATES | |
| --- | --- |
| Sodium-free | Less than 5 milligrams (mg) per serving |
| Very low sodium | 35 mg or less per serving |
| Low sodium | 140 mg or less per serving |
| Light in sodium | At least 50 percent less sodium per serving than average for the same food with no sodium reduction |
| Lightly salted | At least 50 percent less sodium per serving than reference amount. (If the food is not "low in sodium," the statement "not a low sodium food" must appear on the same panel as the "Nutrition Facts" panel.) |
| Reduced or less sodium | At least 25 percent less per serving than reference food |

You should also get used to looking at the list of ingredients, particularly in the case of items that don't have the full nutritional label. This is often the case with items such as spices, which are usually exempt from nutritional labeling because of the small size of the package. In addition to the obvious salt, you should try to avoid any products that contain other sodium compounds such as monosodium glutamate (MSG) and sodium carbonate, which is used as an anticaking additive.

## Notes on Some of the Ingredients Used in the Recipes

This section contains more detailed information on some of the ingredients that you will find in the recipes in this book. This may include how to find the ingredients as well as information on why I've chosen to use a particular item rather than an alternative.

### Butter vs. Margarine

The recipes in this book call for unsalted butter. When I first started the low sodium diet it

seemed a good reason to switch from regular margarine to unsalted butter. It was readily available, sodium-free, and tasted great. It also contains no trans fats, which margarine does. Then my doctor suggested lowering my cholesterol. So I was off on a search for unsalted margarine. It's not as commonly stocked as unsalted butter, but it does exist in several national brands. I've since switched back to butter since my cholesterol is no longer an issue. I also use the I Can't Believe It's Not Butter spray for foods like toast and vegetables. It is still low in sodium and much lower in fat than putting a glob of butter or margarine on something.

### Eggs

Even though the recipes call for eggs, I often use egg substitute instead. I started this as a way to reduce the amount of cholesterol I was taking in, especially since I have eggs for breakfast fairly often. The brand I use does have 25 mg more sodium than whole eggs, so there is a trade-off. If cholesterol isn't an issue for you, it's cheaper and easier to just use whole eggs. I use a store-brand egg substitute that is similar to Egg Beaters. It's basically colored egg whites with some vitamins and minerals. You could also just use egg whites in most of the recipes, but I'm the kind of guy whose mother did too good a job teaching me to clean my plate, and I have a tough time just throwing the yolks away. The "real" whites have more sodium than the yolks do, by the way, so you don't save any sodium by doing that.

## Milk

Although the recipes call for skim milk, there are some lower-sodium alternatives. Some of the liquid nondairy creamers are sodium-free and give you a much richer taste than skim milk. There are also low sodium soy milk products. I've used the nondairy creamer instead of milk myself. I haven't found any recipe where creamer is a problem. The drawback, of course, is that you get none of the nutritional benefits of milk; it is primarily corn syrup and water with some chemicals added. Milk would obviously provide protein and a wide array of vitamins and minerals that my creamer does not. This is not a major concern to me personally because I am careful about getting these nutrients elsewhere, but it is something you should be aware of in making a personal decision to use either the creamer or real milk.

## Baking Powder and Baking Soda

In my humble opinion, this is a no-brainer. If you bake anything that uses baking powder with the regular stuff off your grocer's shelves, you are eating sodium that can easily be avoided. Given the amount of sodium in standard baking powder, it's likely to be 100 to 200 mg per serving. Some doctors also believe the aluminum in regular baking powder is bad for you. The simple solution is sodium-free, aluminum-free baking powder. Several brands are available, but the only one I've

found available locally is Featherweight. I find it at a health food store. It's also available online at Healthy Heart Market and Salt Watcher. The price is also comparable to the regular baking powder.

Like baking powder, regular baking soda is unnecessary sodium intake. The only brand of sodium-free baking soda I'm familiar with is Ener-G, and the only places I've seen it are online at Healthy Heart Market and Salt Watcher. The only thing you need to remember with the sodium-free baking soda is to double the amount called for in your favorite recipes. The recipes in this book already have the amount doubled.

## Seasoning Blends

This covers a whole range of items like seasoned salt, seafood seasoning, taco seasoning, and other blends like Cajun, barbecue, and curry powders. You'll likely be able to find some salt-free versions of these on your regular grocer's shelves. Mrs. Dash makes a number of different blends that are widely available, and major spice manufacturers like McCormick do also. Many spices come in bottles small enough to be exempt from the usual labeling requirements in the United States, so you'll need to read the ingredient list and look for added salt. Health food stores often stock salt-free spice blends, and there are a number of places to get them online. You'll also find recipes for spice blends in Chapter 1: Spice Blends and Seasonings.

## Sauces and Condiments

In looking at products like barbecue sauce, Asian sauces, ketchup, mustard, and salsa, you'll find a wide range of sodium values. Most of the low sodium varieties are made by companies in the organic and specialty foods areas, so you'll have a better chance of finding them in health food stores or markets with large organic food sections. Most of the products you'll find on the regular grocery shelves will contain high amounts of sodium. Low sodium varieties are also available for sale online, or you can make your own using the recipes in Chapter 2: Condiments and Sauces.

## Canned Tomato Products, Vegetables, and Beans

In the United States, more of the large food companies like Hunt's and Del Monte are making these products. I have no trouble finding a good selection of no-salt-added tomato products and a more limited selection of other no-salt-added vegetables in any large supermarket. Beans are less common and are another area where organic food producers are leading the way. With a little more effort you can cook your own dried beans without salt for a fraction of the cost of the canned ones. I usually cook a pound bag at a time and freeze the ones I don't need for future use.

## Soups, Broth, and Bouillon

Like other products, low sodium versions of these are available, but not as widely as might be hoped. Again, organic food producers are the best bet to find a truly low sodium item. There are recipes in Chapter 3: Basic Ingredients for your own stock to replace canned broth. Some very low sodium soup bases from companies like RediBase and Home Again are also available online. These come in a variety of flavors and have a much more natural taste than the sodium-free bouillon cubes.

## Alcohol

Some recipes in this book contain beer, wine, or other alcohol. I realize that these will not be right for everyone. There are any number of good reasons why you might want to avoid alcohol, whether they be medical, religious, or simply that you are cooking for children. And contrary to what we have been told, I've seen several reports that chemically analyzed food containing wine and found that the alcohol does not all burn off or evaporate during cooking. In fact, a sauce made with wine that was simmered for 20 minutes may still contain up to 40 percent of the alcohol. Some alternatives will still let you enjoy the recipes. "Nonalcoholic" beers and wines have had most of the alcohol removed. Typically they contain about one-half of 1 percent alcohol. I've seen it stated that this is about the same as what occurs naturally in orange juice, but I've never seen any conclusive proof of this. You'll have to decide if that is acceptable to you or not. Many of the recipes made with beer or white wine could have chicken broth substituted with no ill effects. For recipes made with red wine, you could replace it with grape juice, adding a few tablespoons of vinegar to counteract the sweetness, although the final flavor may be a little different. In some recipes you may also choose to omit the alcohol. The Bourbon Barbecue Sauce (see page 24) will taste different, but still good, without the whiskey.

### A NOTE ON CHOOSING WINE FOR COOKING

If you decide to use wine in cooking, do not buy the cooking wine in the supermarket. It contains added salt. Legend has it that this practice started on sailing ships, to discourage the cook from drinking the wine instead of adding it to the food. Whatever the reason, you'll want to get your wine for cooking from a liquor store or wine merchant.

## Bread

If you are like most people, one of the biggest single changes that you can make to reduce your sodium intake is to make your own bread. Most commercial bread has well over 100 mg per slice. Many rolls and specialty breads are in the 300 to 400 mg range. A bread machine can reduce the amount of effort required to make your own yeast bread to a manageable level. It takes at most 10 minutes to load it and turn it on. You can even set it on a timer to have your house filled with the aroma of fresh bread when you come home. And you have the satisfaction of knowing that great taste of warm bread is accompanied by a single-digit sodium count. You will read that the salt in bread recipes is required to help control the yeast. Don't believe it! Other than an occasional loaf that has risen too fast and fallen in on top, I've not had a problem. Even in the rare times when that happens, it still tastes just as good.

## Meats

These days, many fresh meats are "enhanced" by injections with a broth solution to make them juicer. Unfortunately, the process also increases the sodium level from 75 to 80 mg per serving to more than 300 mg. This is especially true of chicken and increasingly true of pork also. There is still unadulterated meat around, but you have to be careful and look for it. I've also seen several instances of pork marked "enhanced" that didn't contain a nutrition label to let you know how much sodium had been added.

## Salt Substitutes

You won't find any salt substitutes listed in the ingredients in this book. I know that some people really like them as a way to get that salty flavor without the sodium, but I'm not fond of them

### HOW IS THE NUTRITIONAL INFORMATION CALCULATED?

The nutritional information included with these recipes was calculated using the AccuChef program. It calculates the values using the U.S. Department of Agriculture Standard Reference 16-1 nutritional database, the latest version. I've been using this program since I first started trying to figure out how much sodium was in the recipes I've created. It's inexpensive, easy to use, and has a number of really handy features. For instance, if I go in and change the nutrition figures for an ingredient, it remembers those figures whenever I use that ingredient. So if I find that the listed sodium amount in canned no-salt-added tomatoes is different than the brand I use, I can change it so that it always matches my own brand.

Of course, that implies that these figures are estimates. Every brand of tomatoes, or any other product, is a little different in nutritional content. These figures were calculated using products that I buy here in southern Maryland. If you use a different brand, your nutrition figures may be different. Use the nutritional analysis as a guideline in determining whether a recipe is right for your diet.

myself. There are really two reasons. One is that the potassium chloride they contain tends to have a metallic aftertaste. The other is that I'm concerned that using the substitute will make it harder for your body to adjust to the taste of food without salt. If you are considering using one, you should check with your doctor first to make sure that the increased potassium will not be an issue.

CHAPTER 1

# Spice Blends and Seasonings

---

*Fortunately, the number of salt-free seasoning blends has increased in the past few years. Major spice companies like McCormick now make a number of salt-free blends (look for the bottles with the green caps). Other organic and specialty suppliers make only salt-free seasonings. However, you may not be able to find the spice you are looking for in a salt-free version. Or perhaps you are just out when you needed some. In those cases, making your own spice blends is a simple solution. We have in this chapter a wide variety. You probably won't use all of them. But I hope you discover a few favorites.*

# No-Salt Seasoning

Yield: 46 servings (¼ teaspoon)

*This is one of my favorite variations of a no-salt seasoning mix. It is particularly good with red meats or in soups. The lemon also makes it a good choice for fish.*

1½ teaspoons garlic powder

1¼ teaspoons dried thyme

1¼ teaspoons onion powder

1¼ teaspoons paprika

1¼ teaspoons celery seed

1¼ teaspoons white pepper

1¼ teaspoons dry mustard

1¼ teaspoons dried lemon peel

1¼ teaspoons black pepper

Mix all the ingredients together. Store in an airtight container.

## NUTRITIONAL ANALYSIS

**EACH WITH:** 0 g water; 1 calorie (19% from fat, 15% from protein, 66% from carb); 0 g protein; 0 g total fat; 0 g saturated fat; 0 g monounsaturated fat; 0 g polyunsaturated fat; 0 g carb; 0 g fiber; 0 g sugar; 3 mg calcium; 0 mg iron; 0 mg sodium; 5 mg potassium; 34 IU vitamin A; 0 mg vitamin C; 0 mg cholesterol

## TIP

Use on meats, poultry, and fish.

# Dick's Salt-Free Seasoning

Yield: 22 servings (¼ teaspoon)

*This blend is my attempt to approximate the flavors in the typical seasoned salt blends like Lawry's, without the sodium. It is the latest in a number of variations, and I believe it captures the flavors of the herbs and spices typically used. Use it anywhere seasoned salt is called for or when you want to give food a little extra flavor. I particularly like it in soups and egg dishes.*

1 teaspoon chili powder

¼ teaspoon celery seed

½ teaspoon ground nutmeg

½ teaspoon coriander

1 teaspoon onion powder

1 teaspoon paprika

¼ teaspoon garlic powder

1 teaspoon turmeric

Mix all the ingredients together. Store in an airtight container.

## NUTRITIONAL ANALYSIS

**EACH WITH:** 0 g water; 2 calories (28% from fat, 11% from protein, 60% from carb); 0 g protein; 0 g total fat; 0 g saturated fat; 0 g monounsaturated fat; 0 g polyunsaturated fat; 0 g carb; 0 g fiber; 0 g sugar; 2 mg calcium; 0 mg iron; 0 mg sodium; 10 mg potassium; 90 IU vitamin A; 0 mg vitamin C; 0 mg cholesterol

# Chili Powder

Yield: 14 servings (about 1 teaspoon)

*If you can't find salt-free chili powder ... or if you just like experimenting ... you can easily make your own. Vary the amount of cayenne to match your own idea of how hot chili should be.*

3 teaspoons (7.5 g) paprika

2 teaspoons (2 g) dried oregano

1 teaspoon cumin

1 teaspoon turmeric

1 teaspoon garlic powder

¼ teaspoon cayenne pepper

Mix all the ingredients together. Store in an airtight container.

**NUTRITIONAL ANALYSIS**

**EACH WITH:** 0 g water; 7 calories (27% from fat, 14% from protein, 58% from carb); 0 g protein; 0 g total fat; 0 g saturated fat; 0 g monounsaturated fat; 0 g polyunsaturated fat; 1 g carb; 1 g fiber; 0 g sugar; 7 mg calcium; 1 mg iron; 1 mg sodium; 47 mg potassium; 805 IU vitamin A; 1 mg vitamin C; 0 mg cholesterol

# Curry Powder

Yield: 32 servings (1 teaspoon)

*You can easily fashion your own curry powder to your taste rather than having to be satisfied with what you find on your grocer's shelves. This makes a medium-hot powder, but you can adjust the heat and the proportions of the seasonings however you prefer.*

2 teaspoons (4 g) black pepper

1 teaspoon bay leaf, ground

1 teaspoon cayenne pepper

2 teaspoons (5 g) chili powder

4 teaspoons (8 g) coriander

2 teaspoons (5 g) cumin

4 teaspoons (12 g) garlic powder

1 teaspoon ground allspice

2 teaspoons (5 g) paprika

4 teaspoons (8.8 g) turmeric

Mix all the ingredients together. Store in an airtight container.

**NUTRITIONAL ANALYSIS**

**EACH WITH:** Each with: 0 g water; 6 calories (23% from fat, 14% from protein, 63% from carb); 0 g protein; 0 g total fat; 0 g saturated fat; 0 g monounsaturated fat; 0 g polyunsaturated fat; 1 g carb; 0 g fiber; 0 g sugar; 8 mg calcium; 1 mg iron; 2 mg sodium; 34 mg potassium; 157 IU vitamin A; 1 mg vitamin C; 0 mg cholesterol

# Mexican Seasoning

Yield: 11 servings (1 teaspoon)

*Add to chili, beans, or other Mexican dishes or sprinkle on grilled vegetables like potatoes or onions.*

1 teaspoon dried chile peppers, ground

2 teaspoons (6 g) garlic powder

2 teaspoons (6 g) onion powder

1 teaspoon paprika

1½ teaspoons cumin

1 teaspoon celery seed

1 teaspoon dried oregano

¼ teaspoon cayenne pepper

¼ teaspoon bay leaf, ground

Mix all the ingredients together. Store in an airtight container.

### NUTRITIONAL ANALYSIS

**EACH WITH:** 0 g water; 7 calories (20% from fat, 14% from protein, 65% from carb); 0 g protein; 0 g total fat; 0 g saturated fat; 0 g monounsaturated fat; 0 g polyunsaturated fat; 1 g carb; 0 g fiber; 0 g sugar; 10 mg calcium; 0 mg iron; 1 mg sodium; 28 mg potassium; 193 IU vitamin A; 1 mg vitamin C; 0 mg cholesterol

# Asian Seasoning

Yield: 38 servings (½ teaspoon)

*Add to stir-fries. Also good in salad dressings and dips.*

2 teaspoons (5.4 g) sesame seeds, roasted

1 teaspoon dried onion flakes

1 teaspoon garlic powder

1 teaspoon black pepper

1 teaspoon celery seed

1 teaspoon dried lemon peel

1 teaspoon dry mustard

1 teaspoon bell pepper flakes

Mix all the ingredients together. Store in an airtight container.

### NUTRITIONAL ANALYSIS

**EACH WITH:** 0 g water; 4 calories (49% from fat, 13% from protein, 38% from carb); 0 g protein; 0 g total fat; 0 g saturated fat; 0 g monounsaturated fat; 0 g polyunsaturated fat; 0 g carb; 0 g fiber; 0 g sugar; 7 mg calcium; 0 mg iron; 0 mg sodium; 9 mg potassium; 1 IU vitamin A; 0 mg vitamin C; 0 mg cholesterol

# New Bay Seasoning

Yield: 18 servings (¼ teaspoon)

*Here in Maryland, summer means crabs and other seafood. And seafood means steamed, with Old Bay Seasoning or the locally produced equivalent from the local seafood market. Only trouble is Old Bay contains 330 mg of sodium per ½ teaspoon. So next time you want some steamed seafood, use our low sodium taste-alike substitute.*

1 teaspoon celery seed

1 teaspoon black pepper

½ teaspoon bay leaf, ground

½ teaspoon cardamom

½ teaspoon dry mustard

⅛ teaspoon cloves, ground

1 teaspoon paprika

¼ teaspoon mace

Mix all the ingredients together. Store in an airtight container.

## NUTRITIONAL ANALYSIS

**EACH WITH:** 0 g water; 3 calories (33% from fat, 14% from protein, 53% from carb); 0 g protein; 0 g total fat; 0 g saturated fat; 0 g monounsaturated fat; 0 g polyunsaturated fat; 1 g carb; 0 g fiber; 0 g sugar; 9 mg calcium; 0 mg iron; 1 mg sodium; 14 mg potassium; 70 IU vitamin A; 0 mg vitamin C; 0 mg cholesterol

# Taco Seasoning Mix

Yield: 6 servings (½ teaspoon)

*Several brands of salt-free taco seasoning mix are available, but they aren't always easy to find. Fortunately, it's not difficult to make up your own.*

2 teaspoons (5 g) chili powder

2 teaspoons (6 g) all-purpose flour

2 teaspoons (5 g) cumin

2 teaspoons (2 g) dried oregano

½ teaspoon onion powder

½ teaspoon garlic powder

½ teaspoon cayenne pepper

Combine all ingredients in a resealable plastic bag and shake until completely mixed. Add to browned ground beef along with ½ to ¾ cup (120 to 175 ml) water and cook until reduced to desired consistency.

## NUTRITIONAL ANALYSIS

**EACH WITH:** 1 g water; 23 calories (23% from fat, 12% from protein, 65% from carb); 1 g protein; 1 g total fat; 0 g saturated fat; 0 g monounsaturated fat; 0 g polyunsaturated fat; 4 g carb; 1 g fiber; 0 g sugar; 20 mg calcium; 1 mg iron; 5 mg sodium; 76 mg potassium; 834 IU vitamin A; 2 mg vitamin C; 0 mg cholesterol

# Grill Blend

Yield: 13 servings (1 teaspoon)

*This mixture is good sprinkled on any kind of meat or vegetables before grilling.*

2 teaspoons (2.4 g) dried chile peppers, ground

2 teaspoons (6 g) onion powder

2 teaspoons (6 g) garlic powder

1 teaspoon paprika

1 teaspoon black pepper

1 teaspoon cumin

⅛ teaspoon cayenne pepper

Mix all the ingredients together. Store in an airtight container.

---

**NUTRITIONAL ANALYSIS**

**EACH WITH:** 0 g water; 5 calories (13% from fat, 14% from protein, 72% from carb); 0 g protein; 0 g total fat; 0 g saturated fat; 0 g monounsaturated fat; 0 g polyunsaturated fat; 1 g carb; 0 g fiber; 0 g sugar; 4 mg calcium; 0 mg iron; 1 mg sodium; 24 mg potassium; 197 IU vitamin A; 0 mg vitamin C; 0 mg cholesterol

---

# Memphis Rub

Yield: 11 servings (1 tablespoon)

*A flavorful dry rub for grilled chicken and other meats.*

¼ cup (28 g) paprika

2 teaspoons (10 g) brown sugar

1 teaspoon sugar

1 teaspoon celery seed

1 teaspoon black pepper

2 teaspoons (4 g) cayenne pepper

1 teaspoon dry mustard

1 teaspoon garlic powder

1 teaspoon onion powder

Combine all the ingredients in a jar, twist the lid on tightly, and shake to mix. Store away from heat or light for up to 6 months.

---

**NUTRITIONAL ANALYSIS**

**EACH WITH:** 0 g water; 28 calories (16% from fat, 8% from protein, 76% from carb); 1 g protein; 1 g total fat; 0 g saturated fat; 0 g monounsaturated fat; 0 g polyunsaturated fat; 6 g carb; 1 g fiber; 4 g sugar; 21 mg calcium; 1 mg iron; 3 mg sodium; 94 mg potassium; 1458 IU vitamin A; 2 mg vitamin C; 0 mg cholesterol

---

# Steakhouse Spice Rub

Yield: 4 servings (about 2 teaspoons)

*To give your grilled steaks that steakhouse flavor (without the added salt), rub them with this mixture before putting them on the grill. The sugar helps to create that crispy outer crust and seal in all the juices.*

- 2 teaspoons (6 g) onion powder
- 2 teaspoons (4 g) garlic pepper
- 2 teaspoons (10 g) brown sugar
- 1 teaspoon black pepper, freshly ground

Mix together and rub into meat before cooking.

---

**NUTRITIONAL ANALYSIS**

**EACH WITH:** 0 g water; 19 calories (2% from fat, 8% from protein, 90% from carb); 0 g protein; 0 g total fat; 0 g saturated fat; 0 g monounsaturated fat; 0 g polyunsaturated fat; 5 g carb; 0 g fiber; 3 g sugar; 10 mg calcium; 0 mg iron; 2 mg sodium; 41 mg potassium; 2 IU vitamin A; 1 mg vitamin C; 0 mg cholesterol

# Seafood Boil Blend

Yield: 6 servings

*Use this blend when boiling or steaming seafood or fish.*

- 1 teaspoon mustard seed
- 2 teaspoons (4 g) dill seed
- 1 teaspoon ground ginger
- 1 teaspoon dried chile peppers, crushed
- 1 teaspoon bay leaf, crushed
- ½ teaspoon black pepper
- ½ teaspoon celery seed
- ½ teaspoon ground allspice
- ½ teaspoon ground cinnamon

Mix all the ingredients together. Store in an airtight container. Makes enough to boil 4 to 8 helpings of seafood.

---

**NUTRITIONAL ANALYSIS**

**EACH WITH:** 1 g water; 14 calories (41% from fat, 17% from protein, 43% from carb); 1 g protein; 1 g total fat; 0 g saturated fat; 0 g monounsaturated fat; 0 g polyunsaturated fat; 2 g carb; 1 g fiber; 0 g sugar; 29 mg calcium; 1 mg iron; 1 mg sodium; 33 mg potassium; 44 IU vitamin A; 1 mg vitamin C; 0 mg cholesterol

## TIP

Because this mixture contains whole seeds, it is not as useful to put directly on food.

# Cajun Seasoning

Yield: 24 servings (½ teaspoon)

*Add a little Cajun flavor to your favorite dishes. But leave out the sodium that almost all commercial Cajun seasonings contain.*

- 1 teaspoon paprika
- 2½ teaspoons (3 g) dried onion flakes
- 2 teaspoons (6 g) minced garlic
- 1½ teaspoons dried thyme
- 1 teaspoon marjoram
- ½ teaspoon fennel
- 1 teaspoon cumin
- ½ teaspoon cayenne pepper

Mix all the ingredients together. Store in an airtight container.

**NUTRITIONAL ANALYSIS**

**EACH WITH:** 0 g water; 3 calories (22% from fat, 14% from protein, 65% from carb); 0 g protein; 0 g total fat; 0 g saturated fat; 0 g monounsaturated fat; 0 g polyunsaturated fat; 1 g carb; 0 g fiber; 0 g sugar; 4 mg calcium; 0 mg iron; 0 mg sodium; 14 mg potassium; 172 IU vitamin A; 0 mg vitamin C; 0 mg cholesterol

# Cajun Blackening Spice Mix

Yield: 8 servings (about 1 teaspoon)

*Use this mixture to make blackened fish or chicken.*

- 5 teaspoons (12.5 g) paprika
- 1 teaspoon dried oregano
- 1 teaspoon dried thyme
- 1 teaspoon cayenne pepper
- ½ teaspoon black pepper
- ½ teaspoon white pepper
- ½ teaspoon garlic powder

Mix all the ingredients together. Store in an airtight container.

**NUTRITIONAL ANALYSIS**

**EACH WITH:** 0 g water; 7 calories (25% from fat, 14% from protein, 61% from carb); 0 g protein; 0 g total fat; 0 g saturated fat; 0 g monounsaturated fat; 0 g polyunsaturated fat; 1 g carb; 1 g fiber; 0 g sugar; 8 mg calcium; 1 mg iron; 1 mg sodium; 45 mg potassium; 864 IU vitamin A; 1 mg vitamin C; 0 mg cholesterol

# Jerk Seasoning

Yield: 12 servings (about ½ tablespoon)

*Not as hot as some jerk seasonings you may have had, but hot enough to be interesting.*

- 1 teaspoon onion flakes
- 1 teaspoon onion powder
- 2 teaspoons (2 g) dried thyme
- 1 teaspoon ground allspice
- ¼ teaspoon ground nutmeg
- ¼ teaspoon ground cinnamon
- 2 teaspoons (9 g) sugar
- 1 teaspoon black pepper
- 1 teaspoon cayenne pepper
- 2 teaspoons (1 g) dried chives

Mix together all the ingredients. Store in a tightly closed glass jar.

**NUTRITIONAL ANALYSIS**

**EACH WITH:** 0 g water; 8 calories (8% from fat, 7% from protein, 85% from carb); 0 g protein; 0 g total fat; 0 g saturated fat; 0 g monounsaturated fat; 0 g polyunsaturated fat; 2 g carb; 0 g fiber; 1 g sugar; 9 mg calcium; 0 mg iron; 1 mg sodium; 21 mg potassium; 77 IU vitamin A; 1 mg vitamin C; 0 mg cholesterol

**TIP**

To make an authentic, very hot jerk blend, use powdered Scotch bonnet peppers instead of the cayenne.

# Indian Curry Blend

Yield: 24 servings (about ½ teaspoon)

*Adds a great flavor to vegetable or rice dishes.*

- 1 teaspoon turmeric
- 1 teaspoon coriander
- 2 teaspoons (5 g) paprika
- 1 teaspoon black pepper
- 1 teaspoon cumin
- 1 teaspoon ground ginger
- ½ teaspoon cloves
- ½ teaspoon celery seed
- ½ teaspoon cayenne pepper

Mix all the ingredients together. Store in an airtight container.

**NUTRITIONAL ANALYSIS**

**EACH WITH:** 0 g water; 3 calories (28% from fat, 13% from protein, 59% from carb); 0 g protein; 0 g total fat; 0 g saturated fat; 0 g monounsaturated fat; 0 g polyunsaturated fat; 1 g carb; 0 g fiber; 0 g sugar; 4 mg calcium; 0 mg iron; 1 mg sodium; 20 mg potassium; 122 IU vitamin A; 1 mg vitamin C; 0 mg cholesterol

**TIP**

Moderately hot; adjust the amount of cayenne to your taste.

CHAPTER 2

# Condiments and Sauces

*As with the spice blends in the previous chapter, low sodium varieties of these items are available. But they are often more difficult to find, available only online or in specialty stores. The good news is they are often really easy to make yourself. And you may find that you like the flavor of yours even better than the ones you buy.*

# Barbecue Sauce

Yield: 10 servings

*This is a quick-to-make barbecue sauce that starts with low sodium ketchup. It's toma-toey and relatively sweet, and the spices have a basic chili flavor. In other words, not too different from most bottled sauces.*

½ cup (120 g) low sodium ketchup

½ cup (120 ml) vinegar

½ cup (170 g) honey

¼ cup (85 g) molasses

1 teaspoon chili powder

1 teaspoon onion powder

½ teaspoon garlic powder

1 teaspoon dry mustard

¼ teaspoon cayenne pepper

Combine all ingredients and mix well. Store in a covered jar in the refrigerator.

### NUTRITIONAL ANALYSIS

**EACH WITH:** 24 g water; 97 calories (2% from fat, 2% from protein, 96% from carb); 1 g protein; 0 g total fat; 0 g saturated fat; 0 g monounsaturated fat; 0 g polyunsaturated fat; 25 g carb; 1 g fiber; 22 g sugar; 27 mg calcium; 1 mg iron; 8 mg sodium; 228 mg potassium; 367 IU vitamin A; 3 mg vitamin C; 0 mg cholesterol

# Bourbon Barbecue Sauce

Yield: 8 servings

*This sauce is a variation of one on the back of the Jack Daniel's Wood Smoking Chips bag. It's not very sweet but gives pork or chicken a nice flavor. This sauce should only be used during the last half hour or so or cooking, since it tends to get pretty black and crispy if cooked too long.*

½ cup (120 ml) Jack Daniel's whiskey or other bourbon whiskey

½ cup (120 g) low sodium ketchup

1 teaspoon Worcestershire sauce

2 teaspoons (10 ml) vinegar

½ teaspoon lemon juice

¼ teaspoon garlic powder

½ teaspoon dry mustard

Mix all ingredients together. Brush on meat while cooking.

### NUTRITIONAL ANALYSIS

**EACH WITH:** 23 g water; 52 calories (3% from fat, 5% from protein, 91% from carb); 0 g protein; 0 g total fat; 0 g saturated fat; 0 g monounsaturated fat; 0 g polyunsaturated fat; 5 g carb; 0 g fiber; 4 g sugar; 3 mg calcium; 0 mg iron; 6 mg sodium; 84 mg potassium; 157 IU vitamin A; 4 mg vitamin C; 0 mg cholesterol

# North Carolina Barbecue Sauce

Yield: 16 servings

*This sauce is similar to the ones found in eastern North Carolina. Based on vinegar and red pepper, it tends to be hot and sour but is perfect for a pulled pork sandwich with coleslaw.*

½ cup (120 ml) cider vinegar

½ cup (120 ml) white vinegar

1 teaspoon brown sugar

½ teaspoon cayenne pepper

½ teaspoon hot pepper sauce

½ teaspoon black pepper

Combine the cider vinegar, white vinegar, brown sugar, cayenne pepper, hot pepper sauce, and pepper in a jar or bottle with a tight-fitting lid. Refrigerate for 1 to 2 days before using so that the flavors will blend. Shake occasionally and store for up to 2 months in the refrigerator.

---

### NUTRITIONAL ANALYSIS

**EACH WITH:** 15 g water; 6 calories (4% from fat, 2% from protein, 94% from carb); 0 g protein; 0 g total fat; 0 g saturated fat; 0 g monounsaturated fat; 0 g polyunsaturated fat; 2 g carb; 0 g fiber; 2 g sugar; 2 mg calcium; 0 mg iron; 3 mg sodium; 23 mg potassium; 76 IU vitamin A; 0 mg vitamin C; 0 mg cholesterol

# Chili Sauce

Yield: 48 servings

*I've got to admit I've never been a really big fan of bottled chili sauce. I much prefer the flavor of this chili sauce. There are enough veggies in it to give it something more than a glorified ketchup taste. It keeps well in the refrigerator for weeks, and you could freeze it if you wanted to.*

2 cups (475 ml) no-salt-added tomatoes

8 ounces (230 g) no-salt-added tomato sauce

½ cup (80 g) onion, chopped

½ cup (100 g) sugar

½ cup (50 g) celery, chopped

½ cup (60 g) green bell pepper, chopped

1 teaspoon lemon juice

1 teaspoon brown sugar

1 teaspoon molasses

¼ teaspoon hot pepper sauce

⅛ teaspoon cloves

⅛ teaspoon ground cinnamon

⅛ teaspoon black pepper

⅛ teaspoon dried basil

⅛ teaspoon dried tarragon

½ cup (120 ml) cider vinegar

Combine all ingredients in a large saucepan. Bring to a boil, reduce heat, and simmer uncovered for 1½ hours or until the mixture is reduced to half its original volume.

---

### NUTRITIONAL ANALYSIS

**EACH WITH:** 20 g water; 15 calories (2% from fat, 5% from protein, 94% from carb); 0 g protein; 0 g total fat; 0 g saturated fat; 0 g monounsaturated fat; 0 g polyunsaturated fat; 4 g carb; 0 g fiber; 3 g sugar; 6 mg calcium; 0 mg iron; 3 mg sodium; 56 mg potassium; 39 IU vitamin A; 3 mg vitamin C; 0 mg cholesterol

# Steak Sauce

Yield: 32 servings

*Similar recipes for an A-1–type steak sauce clone show up on a number of websites. This one uses reduced-sodium ingredients to make it applicable to a low sodium diet.*

½ cup (120 ml) orange juice

½ cup (82.5 g) raisins

¼ cup (60 ml) Soy Sauce Substitute (see recipe, page 28)

¼ cup (60 ml) white vinegar

2 teaspoons (10 g) Dijon mustard

¼ cup (60 g) low sodium ketchup

1 teaspoon orange peel, grated

Bring all the ingredients to a boil, then boil for 2 minutes, stirring constantly. Remove from the heat. Allow the mixture to cool to lukewarm. Pour the mixture into a blender and blend until it is smooth. Pour it into a bottle and cap tightly. Refrigerate.

## NUTRITIONAL ANALYSIS

**EACH WITH:** 8 g water; 12 calories (4% from fat, 5% from protein, 91% from carb); 0 g protein; 0 g total fat; 0 g saturated fat; 0 g monounsaturated fat; 0 g polyunsaturated fat; 3 g carb; 0 g fiber; 2 g sugar; 3 mg calcium; 0 mg iron; 1 mg sodium; 39 mg potassium; 25 IU vitamin A; 2 mg vitamin C; 0 mg cholesterol

# Dick's Best Salsa

Yield: 48 servings

*It took me a while, but I finally came up with a recipe for salsa that satisfies me—and I actually wrote down the ingredients while I was concocting it. It passed the taste test when a whole pint jar disappeared into the young people who attended my daughter's college graduation party, so I guess it's okay. This makes a mild version. You could add another chile pepper or two depending on how hot you like it.*

3 pounds (1.4 kg) plum tomatoes, peeled and chopped

½ cup (50 g) black beans, cooked

½ cup (65 g) frozen corn

8 ounces (230 g) no-salt-added tomato sauce

1 chile pepper

¼ cup (60 ml) red wine vinegar

½ cup (80 g) onion, chopped

1 teaspoon minced garlic

1½ teaspoons cilantro

½ teaspoon dried oregano

1½ teaspoons cumin

Combine all ingredients in a large pot. Simmer until desired thickness, about 15 minutes. Pack into jars and store in refrigerator. Makes about 3 pints (1.5 L).

## NUTRITIONAL ANALYSIS

**EACH WITH:** 32 g water; 15 calories (7% from fat, 19% from protein, 74% from carb); 1 g protein; 0 g total fat; 0 g saturated fat; 0 g monounsaturated fat; 0 g polyunsaturated fat; 3 g carb; 1 g fiber; 1 g sugar; 7 mg calcium; 0 mg iron; 2 mg sodium; 110 mg potassium; 254 IU vitamin A; 6 mg vitamin C; 0 mg cholesterol

# Enchilada Sauce

Yield: 16 servings

*This makes a not-too-spicy, tomatoey sauce that is good on tacos as well as a cooking sauce for enchiladas and other baked Mexican dishes.*

1 medium onion, chopped

2 teaspoons (5 g) chili powder

2 teaspoons (10 ml) vegetable oil

2 cups (475 ml) no-salt-added tomatoes

2 cups (475 ml) water

¼ teaspoon cumin

¼ teaspoon garlic powder

Simmer all ingredients together in a saucepan for 1 hour, or until desired thickness.

**NUTRITIONAL ANALYSIS**

**EACH WITH:** 65 g water; 17 calories (36% from fat, 10% from protein, 54% from carb); 0 g protein; 1 g total fat; 0 g saturated fat; 0 g monounsaturated fat; 0 g polyunsaturated fat; 3 g carb; 1 g fiber; 1 g sugar; 14 mg calcium; 0 mg iron; 5 mg sodium; 98 mg potassium; 318 IU vitamin A; 5 mg vitamin C; 0 mg cholesterol

# Fajita Marinade

Yield: 8 servings

*Marinate chicken or beef in this, then grill and slice thinly for easy fajitas. The only other things you need are some sautéed onions and peppers and some low sodium tortillas.*

¼ cup (60 ml) olive oil

¼ cup (60 ml) red wine vinegar

2 teaspoons (10 ml) Worcestershire sauce

2 teaspoons (10 ml) lemon juice

2 teaspoons (10 ml) lime juice

½ teaspoon black pepper

1 teaspoon cilantro

1 teaspoon cumin

1 teaspoon garlic powder

1 teaspoon dried oregano

Mix ingredients together and use to marinate beef or chicken for at least 6 hours or overnight.

**NUTRITIONAL ANALYSIS**

**EACH WITH:** 15 g water; 70 calories (84% from fat, 2% from protein, 14% from carb); 0 g protein; 7 g total fat; 1 g saturated fat; 5 g monounsaturated fat; 1 g polyunsaturated fat; 3 g carb; 0 g fiber; 1 g sugar; 11 mg calcium; 1 mg iron; 17 mg sodium; 69 mg potassium; 47 IU vitamin A; 10 mg vitamin C; 0 mg cholesterol

# Soy Sauce Substitute

Yield: 8 servings

*No, it's not real soy sauce. But I think you might be surprised how little you'll notice the difference from the 300-mg-minimum-per-tablespoon stuff. This was sent to me by a reader of my email newsletter, who said it came from a* Better Homes and Gardens *low sodium cookbook. Ironically, that must be the only book they ever published that I don't have. I usually make a double or triple batch. It keeps well in the refrigerator, and a half a cup never seems to go very far.*

- 2 tablespoons (28 ml) sodium-free beef bouillon
- 2 teaspoons (10 ml) red wine vinegar
- 1 teaspoon molasses
- ⅛ teaspoon ground ginger
- Dash black pepper
- Dash garlic powder
- ¾ cup (175 ml) water

In a small saucepan, combine all ingredients and boil gently, uncovered, for about 5 minutes or until the mixture is reduced to ½ cup (120 ml). Store in the refrigerator. Stir before using.

NUTRITIONAL ANALYSIS

**EACH WITH:** 24 g water; 11 calories (21% from fat, 11% from protein, 68% from carb); 0 g protein; 0 g total fat; 0 g saturated fat; 0 g monounsaturated fat; 0 g polyunsaturated fat; 2 g carb; 0 g fiber; 1 g sugar; 6 mg calcium; 0 mg iron; 22 mg sodium; 21 mg potassium; 10 IU vitamin A; 0 mg vitamin C; 0 mg cholesterol

# Duck Sauce

Yield: 20 servings

*This very low sodium version of the classic Chinese condiment is really simple to make, since it starts with canned preserves.*

- 1 cup (320 g) plum preserves
- ½ cup (160 g) apricot preserves
- 2 tablespoons (40 g) honey
- ⅔ cup (157 ml) cider vinegar
- 1 clove garlic, minced

Mix the ingredients in a saucepan; bring to a boil over medium heat. Cook for 5 minutes, stirring constantly. Store in a sterilized jar in the refrigerator.

NUTRITIONAL ANALYSIS

**EACH WITH:** 16 g water; 72 calories (0% from fat, 1% from protein, 99% from carb); 0 g protein; 0 g total fat; 0 g saturated fat; 0 g monounsaturated fat; 0 g polyunsaturated fat; 18 g carb; 0 g fiber; 15 g sugar; 6 mg calcium; 0 mg iron; 9 mg sodium; 28 mg potassium; 16 IU vitamin A; 2 mg vitamin C; 0 mg cholesterol

# Teriyaki Sauce Substitute

Yield: 20 servings

*A typical Chinese/Japanese condiment that you can make on your own. If you don't have gingerroot, get some … or use ½ teaspoon of ground ginger.*

1 cup (235 ml) Soy Sauce Substitute (see recipe, page 28)

2 teaspoons (10 ml) sesame oil

2 teaspoons (10 ml) sake

½ cup (100 g) sugar

3 cloves garlic, crushed

1 teaspoon gingerroot, minced

Dash black pepper

Combine all ingredients in a saucepan and heat until sugar is dissolved. Store in the refrigerator.

## NUTRITIONAL ANALYSIS

**EACH WITH:** 1 g water; 35 calories (36% from fat, 0% from protein, 63% from carb); 0 g protein; 1 g total fat; 0 g saturated fat; 1 g monounsaturated fat; 1 g polyunsaturated fat; 5 g carb; 0 g fiber; 5 g sugar; 1 mg calcium; 0 mg iron; 0 mg sodium; 4 mg potassium; 0 IU vitamin A; 0 mg vitamin C; 0 mg cholesterol

## TIP

You can substitute sherry or mirin, a sweet Japanese rice wine, for the sake.

# Sweet and Sour Sauce

Yield: 6 servings

*This sauce can be used either on meat and vegetables or as a dipping sauce.*

⅓ cup (80 ml) white vinegar

½ cup (115 g) brown sugar

4 teaspoons (21 g) no-salt-added tomato paste

¾ cup (175 ml) water, divided

2 teaspoons (3 g) cornstarch

Mix together the vinegar, sugar, tomato paste, and ½ cup (120 ml) of the water. Bring to a boil in a small saucepan. Stir together the cornstarch and remaining water. Add to the other ingredients and continue cooking and stirring until thickened.

## NUTRITIONAL ANALYSIS

**EACH WITH:** 51 g water; 90 calories (0% from fat, 2% from protein, 97% from carb); 0 g protein; 0 g total fat; 0 g saturated fat; 0 g monounsaturated fat; 0 g polyunsaturated fat; 23 g carb; 1 g fiber; 20 g sugar; 21 mg calcium; 1 mg iron; 19 mg sodium; 188 mg potassium; 166 IU vitamin A; 2 mg vitamin C; 0 mg

## TIP

If you are adding pineapple to the dish, replace part of the water with the pineapple juice.

# Tartar Sauce

Yield: 24 servings

*A lower-sodium version of this condiment with a flavor that many people seem to prefer to the bottled kind.*

- 1 cup (225 g) low sodium mayonnaise
- ¼ cup (40 g) onion, finely chopped
- ¼ cup (60 g) sweet pickle relish
- ¼ teaspoon black pepper

Combine all ingredients. Allow to stand in the refrigerator several hours or overnight before using.

**NUTRITIONAL ANALYSIS**

**EACH WITH:** 5 g water; 70 calories (92% from fat, 1% from protein, 7% from carb); 0 g protein; 7 g total fat; 1 g saturated fat; 2 g monounsaturated fat; 3 g polyunsaturated fat; 1 g carb; 0 g fiber; 0 g sugar; 2 mg calcium; 0 mg iron; 24 mg sodium; 6 mg potassium; 30 IU vitamin A; 0 mg vitamin C; 5 mg cholesterol

# Mustard

Yield: 36 servings

*This makes a good general-purpose kind of mustard.*

- ¼ cup (36 g) dry mustard
- ¼ cup (60 ml) white wine vinegar
- ¼ cup (60 ml) white wine
- 1 teaspoon sugar
- 1 egg yolk

Blend together all the ingredients except the egg yolk and let stand for 2 hours. Beat the egg yolk into the mixture. Cook, stirring constantly, until slightly thickened, about 5 minutes. Store covered in the refrigerator.

**NUTRITIONAL ANALYSIS**

**EACH WITH:** Each with: 7 g water; 5 calories (29% from fat, 36% from protein, 35% from carb); 0 g protein; 0 g total fat; 0 g saturated fat; 0 g monounsaturated fat; 0 g polyunsaturated fat; 0 g carb; 0 g fiber; 0 g sugar; 3 mg calcium; 0 mg iron; 5 mg sodium; 14 mg potassium; 12 IU vitamin A; 0 mg vitamin C; 0 mg cholesterol

**TIP**

If you like mustard less hot, heat the vinegar to almost boiling before mixing the ingredients together.

# Spicy Brown Mustard

Yield: 96 servings

*Mustard is one of those things that typically has added salt but doesn't seem to suffer from the lack of it. This particular mustard is similar to the coarse-ground French mustard like Grey Poupon Country French.*

⅓ cup (59 g) mustard seeds

⅓ cup (48 g) dry mustard

⅔ cup (157 ml) water, boiling

1 cup (235 ml) cider vinegar

3 teaspoons (15 ml) light corn syrup

2 teaspoons (10 g) brown sugar

1 teaspoon onion powder

½ teaspoon garlic powder

½ teaspoon ground cinnamon

¼ teaspoon ground allspice

⅛ teaspoon ground cloves

In a small bowl, combine the mustard seeds, dry mustard, and boiling water. Stir to mix and set aside for 10 minutes. In a saucepan, combine the remaining ingredients and bring to a boil. Reduce the heat and simmer, covered, for 5 minutes. Remove from heat. Place mustard and vinegar mixtures in a blender and process at high speed until seeds are crushed. Place in a pint jar and store in the refrigerator. Can be used immediately.

## NUTRITIONAL ANALYSIS

**EACH WITH:** 4 g water; 7 calories (26% from fat, 11% from protein, 63% from carb); 0 g protein; 0 g total fat; 0 g saturated fat; 0 g monounsaturated fat; 0 g polyunsaturated fat; 1 g carb; 0 g fiber; 1 g sugar; 5 mg calcium; 0 mg iron; 1 mg sodium; 10 mg potassium; 1 IU vitamin A; 0 mg vitamin C; 0 mg cholesterol

# Honey Mustard Sauce

Yield: 4 servings

*You can use this when grilling either fish, chicken, or pork to give a sweet and slightly spicy taste.*

¼ cup (85 g) honey

2 teaspoons (10 ml) cider vinegar

2 teaspoons (10 g) mustard

½ teaspoon onion powder

¼ teaspoon garlic powder

Mix ingredients together. Brush over meat when grilling or roasting.

## NUTRITIONAL ANALYSIS

**EACH WITH:** 17 g water; 72 calories (3% from fat, 2% from protein, 95% from carb); 0 g protein; 0 g total fat; 0 g saturated fat; 0 g monounsaturated fat; 0 g polyunsaturated fat; 19 g carb; 0 g fiber; 18 g sugar; 9 mg calcium; 0 mg iron; 4 mg sodium; 35 mg potassium; 10 IU vitamin A; 0 mg vitamin C; 0 mg cholesterol

# Roasted Garlic

Yield: 8 servings

*Roasted garlic is the hot new ingredient in packaged mixes as well as restaurant menus. It adds a mild garlic flavor without being overpowering. And it's easy to make at home, even without one of the clay garlic roasters that you'll see advertised.*

1 whole garlic pod
1 tablespoon (15 ml) olive oil

Hold pod of garlic on the side, take a sharp knife, and cut the pod about ¼ inch (0.64 cm) from the top all the way across, exposing the raw garlic cloves. Place on a baking sheet covered with aluminum foil. Pour and rub in olive oil in to the top of the garlic. Bake in a 325°F (170°C, gas mark 3) oven for 45 minutes to 1 hour or until garlic is soft; remove and let cool. Separate each garlic clove from the pod and pinch at the stem end to remove the garlic paste. Cover and refrigerate.

**NUTRITIONAL ANALYSIS**

**EACH WITH:** 0 g water; 15 calories (96% from fat, 1% from protein, 3% from carb); 0 g protein; 2 g total fat; 0 g saturated fat; 1 g monounsaturated fat; 0 g polyunsaturated fat; 0 g carb; 0 g fiber; 0 g sugar; 1 mg calcium; 0 mg iron; 0 mg sodium; 1 mg potassium; 0 IU vitamin A; 0 mg vitamin C; 0 mg cholesterol

# Basil Pesto

Yield: 12 servings

*This makes a fairly typical pesto, but without the usual added salt.*

2 cups (80 g) fresh basil, packed
3 teaspoons (9 g) pine nuts
3 cloves garlic, finely minced
¼ cup (25 g) Parmesan cheese, grated
½ cup (120 ml) olive oil

Place basil leaves in small batches in food processor and whip until well chopped (do about ¾ cup [30 g] at a time). Add about ⅓ of the nuts and garlic; blend again. Add about ⅓ of the Parmesan cheese; blend while slowly adding about ⅓ of the olive oil, stopping to scrape down sides of container. Process basil pesto until it forms a thick, smooth paste. Repeat until all ingredients are used; mix all batches together well. Serve over pasta. Basil pesto keeps in refrigerator 1 week, or freeze for a few months.

**NUTRITIONAL ANALYSIS**

**EACH WITH:** 1 g water; 116 calories (81% from fat, 6% from protein, 13% from carb); 2 g protein; 11 g total fat; 2 g saturated fat; 7 g monounsaturated fat; 2 g polyunsaturated fat; 4 g carb; 2 g fiber; 0 g sugar; 141 mg calcium; 3 mg iron; 31 mg sodium; 209 mg potassium; 536 IU vitamin A; 4 mg vitamin C; 1 mg cholesterol

# Cucumber Raita

Yield: 6 servings

*No Indian meal is complete without raita. Use this cool condiment to dip your naan in or just as a way to cool off the heat of a spicy meal.*

1 cucumber, peeled and chopped

1 cup (230 g) plain low-fat yogurt

½ cup (15 g) mint leaves, fresh

2 teaspoons (10 ml) lime juice

Combine the ingredients and refrigerate for several hours before serving.

### NUTRITIONAL ANALYSIS

**EACH WITH:** 90 g water; 36 calories (17% from fat, 27% from protein, 56% from carb); 3 g protein; 1 g total fat; 0 g saturated fat; 0 g monounsaturated fat; 0 g polyunsaturated fat; 5 g carb; 1 g fiber; 4 g sugar; 91 mg calcium; 1 mg iron; 31 mg sodium; 192 mg potassium; 230 IU vitamin A; 4 mg vitamin C; 2 mg cholesterol

# Sun-Dried Tomato Vinaigrette

Yield: 8 servings

*Nice flavor—and a fair amount of fat, which I've not made any attempt to reduce.*

3 teaspoons (15 ml) white wine vinegar

¼ cup (14 g) sun-dried tomatoes, chopped

1 teaspoon Worcestershire sauce

1 clove garlic, minced

½ teaspoon sugar

¼ teaspoon white pepper

⅓ cup (80 ml) olive oil

Shake all ingredients together in a jar with a tight-fitting lid.

### NUTRITIONAL ANALYSIS

**EACH WITH:** 8 g water; 90 calories (91% from fat, 1% from protein, 8% from carb); 0 g protein; 9 g total fat; 1 g saturated fat; 7 g monounsaturated fat; 1 g polyunsaturated fat; 2 g carb; 0 g fiber; 1 g sugar; 3 mg calcium; 0 mg iron; 12 mg sodium; 66 mg potassium; 45 IU vitamin A; 5 mg vitamin C; 0 mg cholesterol

# CHAPTER 3

# Basic Ingredients

*Now we come to a group of items that are generally not available at all in low sodium versions. Yes, you may find a few low sodium pickles or broth that is not too high in sodium. But if you really want low sodium croutons, or condensed soup, or baking mix, you are going to have to make them yourself. Fortunately, it's most often a pretty simple procedure to do so. And it enables you to have things that you would otherwise have to give up.*

# Cream Soup Mix

Yield: 18 servings

*A soup base for making your own condensed cream soups. One recipe makes enough for the equivalent of nine cans of soup.*

- 2 cups (220 g) nonfat dry milk powder
- ¾ cup (96 g) cornstarch
- 2 tablespoons (28 ml) low sodium chicken bouillon
- 1 tablespoon (9 g) onion flakes
- ¼ teaspoon dried thyme
- ¼ teaspoon dried basil
- ¼ teaspoon black pepper

Combine all ingredients in a food processor. Mix well until the dehydrated onion pieces are no longer visible. Store in an airtight container.

### NUTRITIONAL ANALYSIS

**EACH WITH:** 1 g water; 52 calories (3% from fat, 22% from protein, 75% from carb); 3 g protein; 0 g total fat; 0 g saturated fat; 0 g monounsaturated fat; 0 g polyunsaturated fat; 10 g carb; 0 g fiber; 4 g sugar; 96 mg calcium; 0 mg iron; 51 mg sodium; 137 mg potassium; 185 IU vitamin A; 1 mg vitamin C; 1 mg cholesterol

### TIP

To make Condensed Cream of Chicken Soup—Blend ⅓ cup (33 g) mix and 1¼ cups (295 ml) chicken broth in a 1-quart (1-L) saucepan or microwave-safe dish until smooth. Bring to a boil or microwave for 2½ to 3 minutes. Stir occasionally; cool. For Condensed Cream of Mushroom soup, add ½ cup (35 g) mushrooms. For Condensed Cream of Celery soup, add ½ cup (50 g) sliced celery.

# Chicken Stock

Yield: 8 servings

*This homemade broth is at least as flavorful as the low sodium canned stuff and a lot lower in sodium. You could also make your own version of the fancier broths now available by adding a couple of cloves of garlic or a tablespoon of Italian seasoning. The chicken can be used in other recipes calling for cooked chicken or for things like chicken salad sandwiches. The 8 servings represent about a cup of broth once diluted.*

- 1 onion
- 1 cup (130 g) carrot
- 1 cup (100 g) celery
- 1 chicken (4 lbs [1.8 kg])
- ½ cup (120 ml) water

Slice veggies and place in bottom of slow cooker. Put chicken on top, breast side up. You can also use leg quarters, necks, and backs or whatever is cheap. Pour water over. Cook on low for 8 to 9 hours. Remove chicken from pot and let cool until easy to handle. Remove chicken from bones and cut up as needed. Remove veggies from broth and discard. Cool broth in refrigerator and remove fat from top. Broth may be mixed with an equal amount of water and used in any recipe calling for chicken broth. Both chicken and broth may be frozen until needed.

### NUTRITIONAL ANALYSIS

**EACH WITH:** 61 g water; 30 calories (22% from fat, 31% from protein, 47% from carb); 2 g protein; 1 g total fat; 0 g saturated fat; 0 g monounsaturated fat; 0 g polyunsaturated fat; 4 g carb; 1 g fiber; 2 g sugar; 16 mg calcium; 0 mg iron; 31 mg sodium; 130 mg potassium; 1998 IU vitamin A; 2 mg vitamin C; 7 mg cholesterol

# Beef Stock

Yield: 8 servings

*As with the chicken stock recipe, this produces broth that can be diluted before using. It cooks easily in the slow cooker and gives you a good-size quantity of broth, plus beef that can be used for soup, barbecued beef sandwiches, or other uses. If you don't need all the broth, package it up in 2-cup freezer containers that can be thawed and used in place of a can of beef broth.*

1 onion

2 carrots

1 cup (100 g) celery

1½ pounds (680 g) beef chuck

1½ cups (355 ml) water

½ teaspoon black pepper

1 teaspoon dried thyme

Slice veggies and place in bottom of slow cooker. Cut up beef and place on top. Pour water over. Add spices. Cook on low for 8 to 9 hours. Remove meat from pot and let cool until easy to handle. Remove beef from bones and cut up as needed. Remove veggies from broth and discard. Cool broth in refrigerator and remove fat from top. Broth may be mixed with equal amount of water and used in any recipe calling for beef broth. Both beef and broth may be frozen until needed.

## NUTRITIONAL ANALYSIS

**EACH WITH:** 90 g water; 79 calories (63% from fat, 26% from protein, 11% from carb); 5 g protein; 6 g total fat; 2 g saturated fat; 2 g monounsaturated fat; 0 g polyunsaturated fat; 2 g carb; 1 g fiber; 1 g sugar; 16 mg calcium; 1 mg iron; 33 mg sodium; 140 mg potassium; 73 IU vitamin A; 2 mg vitamin C; 20 mg cholesterol

# Vegetable Stock

Yield: 6 servings

*It's fairly easy to make your own low sodium vegetable broth. Feel free to vary the amount and type of vegetables to get a flavor you like. Potato peels can be included if you have any, as can a sweet potato or mushrooms. I picked the ones I used for a combination of flavor and low cost. Strong-flavored vegetables such as tomatoes and cabbage can overwhelm the others, so use them sparingly unless you are after a broth that is primarily tomato flavored. If you use a strainer like the ones sold to cook pasta, it simplifies the straining.*

2 quarts (2-L) water

½ cup (50 g) celery, sliced

¾ cup (98 g) carrot, sliced

1 onion, quartered

2 turnips, quartered

1 cup (20 g) spinach

2 leeks, sliced

1 tablespoon (5 g) peppercorns

1 bay leaf

½ cup (30 g) fresh parsley

Combine all ingredients in a large stockpot and simmer for 2 hours. Strain and use as needed. May be frozen.

## NUTRITIONAL ANALYSIS

**EACH WITH:** 447 g water; 57 calories (5% from fat, 11% from protein, 84% from carb); 2 g protein; 0 g total fat; 0 g saturated fat; 0 g monounsaturated fat; 0 g polyunsaturated fat; 13 g carb; 3 g fiber; 5 g sugar; 72 mg calcium; 2 mg iron; 80 mg sodium; 345 mg potassium; 3359 IU vitamin A; 27 mg vitamin C; 0 mg cholesterol

# Fish Stock

Yield: 8 servings

*Used to make Chinese soups or fish sauce.*

1 pound (455 g) fish bones, heads and tails

4 cups (940 ml) low sodium chicken broth

1 onion, minced

¼ cup (25 g) scallion, chopped

¼ teaspoon black pepper

2 tablespoons (28 ml) cider vinegar

2 tablespoons (4 g) dried cilantro

2 tablespoons (28 ml) low sodium chicken bouillon

In a wok or Dutch oven, combine the first 6 ingredients. Bring to a boil, add the cilantro, cover, and simmer for a half hour. Stir in bouillon, cover, and simmer for 10 minutes more. Strain and store in refrigerator.

### NUTRITIONAL ANALYSIS

**EACH WITH:** 37 g water; 29 calories (9% from fat, 55% from protein, 36% from carb); 4 g protein; 0 g total fat; 0 g saturated fat; 0 g monounsaturated fat; 0 g polyunsaturated fat; 3 g carb; 0 g fiber; 1 g sugar; 11 mg calcium; 0 mg iron; 80 mg sodium; 129 mg potassium; 122 IU vitamin A; 3 mg vitamin C; 10 mg cholesterol

### TIP

If you don't have fish bones, etc., to put in, use a pound of fish instead.

# Tempura Batter

Yield: 6 servings

*This makes a fairly thin batter that can be used either for meat like fish, chicken, or shrimp or for vegetables.*

2 eggs

1¾ cups (410 ml) water, very cold

1¾ cups (185 g) all-purpose flour

Beat eggs and water until frothy. Beat in flour until batter is smooth. Refrigerate until ready to use. Place batter in a bowl of crushed ice to keep cold while using.

### NUTRITIONAL ANALYSIS

**EACH WITH:** 91 g water; 150 calories (6% from fat, 17% from protein, 76% from carb); 6 g protein; 1 g total fat; 0 g saturated fat; 0 g monounsaturated fat; 0 g polyunsaturated fat; 28 g carb; 1 g fiber; 0 g sugar; 18 mg calcium; 2 mg iron; 39 mg sodium; 108 mg potassium; 75 IU vitamin A; 0 mg vitamin C; 0 mg cholesterol

# Brown Gravy Mix

Yield: 24 servings

*Yes, it says instant coffee. Don't be afraid— the coffee doesn't really make this mix taste weird. And it certainly does give it that nice brown color.*

1⅔ cups (204 g) cornstarch

6 tablespoons (90 ml) low sodium beef bouillon

4 teaspoons instant coffee crystals

2 teaspoons (6 g) onion powder

1 teaspoon garlic powder

½ teaspoon black pepper

½ teaspoon paprika

Combine all ingredients and store in an airtight container. To make gravy, measure 3 tablespoons (21 g) mix into a saucepan. Add 1½ cups (355 ml) water. Bring to a boil and simmer for 1 minute.

**NUTRITIONAL ANALYSIS**

**EACH WITH:** 1 g water; 36 calories (1% from fat, 1% from protein, 98% from carb); 0 g protein; 0 g total fat; 0 g saturated fat; 0 g monounsaturated fat; 0 g polyunsaturated fat; 8 g carb; 0 g fiber; 0 g sugar; 2 mg calcium; 0 mg iron; 22 mg sodium; 11 mg potassium; 25 IU vitamin A; 0 mg vitamin C; 0 mg cholesterol

# Seasoned Bread Crumbs

Yield: 4 servings

*Next time you are looking for a low sodium topping to add a little crunch and flavor to a casserole or some veggies, give this a try.*

½ cup (60 g) low sodium bread crumbs

1 teaspoon brown sugar

½ teaspoon sesame seeds

1 teaspoon wheat germ

½ teaspoon celery seed

½ teaspoon dried oregano

¼ teaspoon garlic powder

1 teaspoon minced onion

½ teaspoon dried parsley

1 teaspoon Italian seasoning

1½ teaspoons buttermilk powder

Combine all ingredients and mix well.

**NUTRITIONAL ANALYSIS**

**EACH WITH:** 1 g water; 72 calories (13% from fat, 15% from protein, 72% from carb); 3 g protein; 1 g total fat; 0 g saturated fat; 0 g monounsaturated fat; 0 g polyunsaturated fat; 13 g carb; 1 g fiber; 3 g sugar; 50 mg calcium; 1 mg iron; 11 mg sodium; 81 mg potassium; 41 IU vitamin A; 1 mg vitamin C; 1 mg cholesterol

**TIP**

This can be made in bigger batches and stored indefinitely in the freezer.

# Croutons

Yield: 4 servings

*Make your own seasoned croutons for your salads and save all the sodium and a good bit of the fat. Feel free to vary the seasonings to suit your taste.*

- 2 tablespoons (30 ml) olive oil
- ½ teaspoon garlic powder
- ½ teaspoon onion powder
- ¼ teaspoon dried thyme
- ¼ teaspoon dried basil
- ½ teaspoon dried parsley
- 2 cups low sodium bread, cubed

Place oil and spices in a resealable plastic bag and mix well. Add bread cubes and shake to coat evenly. Place in a single layer on a greased baking sheet and bake at 300°F (150°C, gas mark 2) until dried out, about 20 minutes, stirring occasionally.

**NUTRITIONAL ANALYSIS**

**EACH WITH:** 8 g water; 122 calories (56% from fat, 6% from protein, 38% from carb); 2 g protein; 8 g total fat; 1 g saturated fat; 5 g monounsaturated fat; 1 g polyunsaturated fat; 12 g carb; 1 g fiber; 1 g sugar; 28 mg calcium; 1 mg iron; 7 mg sodium; 36 mg potassium; 20 IU vitamin A; 0 mg vitamin C; 0 mg cholesterol

**TIP**

Italian bread works well for this recipe.

# Buttermilk Baking Mix

Yield: 26 servings

*Use this mix in any recipe that calls for a boxed baking mix.*

- 10½ cups (1155 g) all-purpose flour
- ¼ cup (55 g) sodium-free baking powder
- ½ cup (100 g) sugar
- 1 cup (110 g) buttermilk powder
- 1½ teaspoons sodium-free baking soda
- 2 cups (400 g) shortening

In a large bowl, mix all ingredients with an electric mixer until particles are small and uniform in size. Store in a tightly covered container.

**NUTRITIONAL ANALYSIS**

**EACH WITH:** 6 g water; 358 calories (41% from fat, 8% from protein, 51% from carb); 7 g protein; 17 g total fat; 4 g saturated fat; 7 g monounsaturated fat; 4 g polyunsaturated fat; 46 g carb; 1 g fiber; 6 g sugar; 162 mg calcium; 3 mg iron; 27 mg sodium; 361 mg potassium; 8 IU vitamin A; 0 mg vitamin C; 3 mg cholesterol

# Granola

Yield: 22 servings

*If you can't find salt-free granola in your local store, it's not difficult to make. You can use this as either cold or hot cereal or in other recipes like muffins and cookies. It also makes a good topping for fruit or yogurt (or ice cream). It does tend to get stale, though, so if you can't use it all in a couple weeks, keep it in a plastic bag in the freezer.*

6 cups (480 g) quick-cooking oats

1½ cups (168 g) wheat germ

1 cup unsalted nuts

1 cup dried fruit

1 cup (225 g) sunflower seeds, unsalted

½ cup (35 g) coconut

½ cup (120 ml) vegetable oil

½ cup (170 g) honey

¼ cup (85 g) molasses

1 tablespoon (15 ml) vanilla extract

2 teaspoons (5 g) ground cinnamon

1 teaspoon ground nutmeg

Combine all ingredients. Bake in an ungreased 13 x 9-inch (33 x 23-cm) pan at 350°F (180°C, gas mark 4) for 20 to 25 minutes, stirring frequently. Cool. Stir until crumbled. Store in an airtight container.

## NUTRITIONAL ANALYSIS

**EACH WITH:** 7 g water; 353 calories (38% from fat, 12% from protein, 50% from carb); 11 g protein; 15 g total fat; 3 g saturated fat; 5 g monounsaturated fat; 7 g polyunsaturated fat; 45 g carb; 7 g fiber; 9 g sugar; 46 mg calcium; 3 mg iron; 5 mg sodium; 407 mg potassium; 3 IU vitamin A; 0 mg vitamin C; 0 mg cholesterol

# Mayonnaise

Yield: 20 servings

*Yes, you can make your own mayonnaise. It's not difficult at all and the flavor is great, perfect with fresh tomatoes. The other good news is that even though the fat content is as high as commercial mayo, the sodium is well below anything that I can find here locally. Although most recipes call for whole eggs or egg yolks, egg substitute can be used successfully instead. This avoids the issue of potential salmonella poisoning with raw eggs. If you prefer, you can also look for eggs that have been irradiated, making them safe to eat raw.*

1 egg, or ¼ cup egg substitute

1 teaspoon Dijon mustard

½ teaspoon white pepper

1½ teaspoons white wine vinegar

1 cup (235 ml) corn oil

2 tablespoons (28 ml) lemon juice

Place everything but the oil and lemon juice in the blender or food processor container. Process 5 seconds in the blender or 15 seconds in the processor. With the motor running, add the oil, first in a drizzle, then in a thin, steady stream. When all the oil has been added, stop the motor and taste. Add lemon juice to your taste. If the sauce is too thick, thin with hot water or lemon juice. If too thin, process a little longer.

## NUTRITIONAL ANALYSIS

**EACH WITH:** 4 g water; 101 calories (98% from fat, 1% from protein, 1% from carb); 0 g protein; 11 g total fat; 1 g saturated fat; 3 g monounsaturated fat; 6 g polyunsaturated fat; 0 g carb; 0 g fiber; 0 g sugar; 2 mg calcium; 0 mg iron; 4 mg sodium; 7 mg potassium; 15 IU vitamin A; 1 mg vitamin C; 12 mg cholesterol

# Mixed Pickles

Yield: 32 servings

*Sweet, bread and butter–style pickles. You can also add other vegetables if you like.*

1 cup (135 g) cucumber, cubed

1 onion, sliced

½ cup (130 g) carrot, sliced

½ cup (60 g) red bell pepper, cubed

1 cup (150 g) cauliflower, cut up

½ cup zucchini, cubed

½ cup (35 g) broccoli, cut up

1¼ cups (295 ml) cider vinegar

1¼ cups (250 g) sugar

½ teaspoon turmeric

½ teaspoon mustard seed

½ teaspoon celery seed

Slice chilled vegetables. Cover and refrigerate. In a saucepan, combine vinegar, sugar, and spices. Heat to boiling. Add cucumber mixture. Heat 2 to 3 minutes. Chill and serve. May be stored in the refrigerator for 1 month. For longer storage, sterilize 2 pint jars. Pack hot pickles to within ½ inch (4 cm) of top. Wipe off rim, screw on top, and place in Dutch oven or other deep pan. Cover with water, bring to a boil, and cook for 10 minutes.

## NUTRITIONAL ANALYSIS

**EACH WITH:** 26 g water; 38 calories (2% from fat, 3% from protein, 96% from carb); 0 g protein; 0 g total fat; 0 g saturated fat; 0 g monounsaturated fat; 0 g polyunsaturated fat; 10 g carb; 0 g fiber; 9 g sugar; 6 mg calcium; 0 mg iron; 3 mg sodium; 45 mg potassium; 317 IU vitamin A; 6 mg vitamin C; 0 mg cholesterol

# Refrigerator Sweet Pickles

Yield: 36 servings

*These make a very good salt-free pickle. They are sweeter than a traditional dill pickle, but not as sweet as most bread and butter recipes. The best part is they are never "cooked" so they stay nice and crispy.*

2 cups (400 g) sugar

2 cups (475 ml) white wine vinegar

1½ cups (355 ml) red wine vinegar

1½ cups (355 ml) cider vinegar

4 tablespoons (12 g) dill weed

1 teaspoon black pepper

2 teaspoons (4 g) celery seed

½ teaspoon dry mustard

1 teaspoon turmeric

5 cucumbers, sliced

Combine all ingredients except cucumbers. Stir until sugar is dissolved. Put cucumbers in jars and pour liquid over. Put lids on and store in refrigerator. Will keep for up to 9 months.

## NUTRITIONAL ANALYSIS

**EACH WITH:** 71 g water; 56 calories (1% from fat, 2% from protein, 96% from carb); 0 g protein; 0 g total fat; 0 g saturated fat; 0 g monounsaturated fat; 0 g polyunsaturated fat; 15 g carb; 0 g fiber; 14 g sugar; 17 mg calcium; 1 mg iron; 2 mg sodium; 111 mg potassium; 64 IU vitamin A; 1 mg vitamin C; 0 mg cholesterol

# Refrigerator Dill Pickles

Yield: 12 servings

*Low sodium dill pickles are more difficult to make than sweet pickles. The salt solution they are typically soaked in helps to keep the pickles crisp. The overnight soaking in cold water helps to solve this problem. I've also found that using small whole pickling cucumbers gives you a crisper pickle than sliced cucumbers. You can always slice them for your favorite sandwiches when you serve them.*

12 small cucumbers

1 tablespoon (6.5 g) dill seed

1 teaspoon whole pickling spice

2 cloves garlic

¾ teaspoon alum

2½ cups (570 ml) water

1½ cups (355 ml) cider vinegar

1 teaspoon sugar

Rinse cucumbers and soak overnight in cold water. Dry and place in a sterilized quart jar. Add dill, pickling spice, garlic, and alum to the jar. In a saucepan, heat water, vinegar, and sugar to a boil. Pour boiling liquid into jar to within ½ inch (1¼ cm) of the top. Put lids on and store in refrigerator. Keep at least 2 weeks before serving.

**NUTRITIONAL ANALYSIS**

**EACH WITH:** 364 g water; 56 calories (5% from fat, 12% from protein, 83% from carb); 2 g protein; 0 g total fat; 0 g saturated fat; 0 g monounsaturated fat; 0 g polyunsaturated fat; 14 g carb; 2 g fiber; 8 g sugar; 60 mg calcium; 1 mg iron; 7 mg sodium; 481 mg potassium; 316 IU vitamin A; 9 mg vitamin C; 0 mg cholesterol

# Tahini

Yield: 8 servings

*Useful for making hummus and other Greek and Middle Eastern recipes.*

2 tablespoons (16 g) sesame seeds

½ cup (120 ml) sesame oil

¼ cup (60 ml) water, tepid

Blend sesame seeds in a blender and grind until smooth. Add sesame oil, then slowly add water while blending. Blend until completely smooth.

**NUTRITIONAL ANALYSIS**

**EACH WITH:** 7 g water; 120 calories (100% from fat, 0% from protein, 0% from carb); 0 g protein; 14 g total fat; 2 g saturated fat; 5 g monounsaturated fat; 6 g polyunsaturated fat; 0 g carb; 0 g fiber; 0 g sugar; 0 mg calcium; 0 mg iron; 0 mg sodium; 0 mg potassium; 0 IU vitamin A; 0 mg vitamin C; 0 mg cholesterol

# CHAPTER 4

# Appetizers, Snacks, and Party Foods

---

*Looking for a way to truly amaze your friends? Throw a party and have a table full of these appetizers, then tell them that they are all low sodium. They won't believe you. Or maybe just please your family with some warm, flavorful, sodium-free tortilla or potato chips. These recipes prove that you can have low sodium snacks that taste good.*

# Buffalo Wings

Yield: 16 servings (3 wing peices per serving)

*An almost traditional Buffalo wings recipe. These are not deep fried, but cooked in the oven, reducing the amount of fat while still allowing them to get crispy. McIlhenny's Original Tabasco Sauce is the lowest-sodium hot pepper sauce that I've seen in local gro-ceries. It has only 30 mg per teaspoon, while most of the others have 5 to 10 times that.*

24 chicken wings
3 tablespoons (45 g) unsalted butter
3 tablespoons hot pepper sauce
2 tablespoons (30 ml) white vinegar

Cut off and discard the small tip of each wing. Cut the main wing bone and second wing bone at the joint. Place in a roasting pan and roast in 350°F (180°C, gas mark 4) oven until crisp, 30 to 40 minutes. Melt butter in small saucepan; add the hot pepper sauce and vinegar. Place wings in a large bowl with a tight-sealing cover. Pour butter mixture over the wings and shake to coat. Remove wings, allowing extra sauce to drain.

### NUTRITIONAL ANALYSIS

**EACH WITH:** 17 g water; 59 calories (58% from fat, 41% from protein, 1% from carb); 6 g protein; 4 g total fat; 2 g saturated fat; 1 g monounsaturated fat; 0 g polyunsaturated fat; 0 g carb; 0 g fiber; 0 g sugar; 4 mg calcium; 0 mg iron; 35 mg sodium; 47 mg potassium; 122 IU vitamin A; 0 mg vitamin C; 22 mg cholesterol

# Spicy Potato Skins

Yield: 24 servings

*These tasty potato skins are lower in fat than the "original" version because they are baked and not fried.*

4 potatoes
¼ cup (60 ml) olive oil
1½ teaspoons coriander
½ teaspoon black pepper
1½ teaspoons chili powder
1½ teaspoons curry powder

Preheat the oven to 400°F (200°C, gas mark 6). Bake the potatoes for 1 hour. Remove the potatoes from the oven, but keep the oven on. Slice the potatoes in half lengthwise and let them cool for 10 minutes. Scoop out most of the potato flesh, leaving about ¼ inch (0.64 cm) of flesh against the potato skin (you can save the potato flesh for another use, like mashed potatoes). Cut each potato half crosswise into 3 pieces. Place the olive oil in a small cup. Dip each potato piece into the olive oil and place it on a baking sheet. Combine the spices and sprinkle the mixture over the potatoes. Bake the potato skins for 15 minutes or until they are crispy and brown.

### NUTRITIONAL ANALYSIS

**EACH WITH:** 39 g water; 64 calories (32% from fat, 6% from protein, 62% from carb); 1 g protein; 2 g total fat; 0 g saturated fat; 2 g monounsaturated fat; 0 g polyunsaturated fat; 10 g carb; 1 g fiber; 0 g sugar; 6 mg calcium; 0 mg iron; 3 mg sodium; 171 mg potassium; 51 IU vitamin A; 4 mg vitamin C; 0 mg cholesterol

# Spinach Dip

Yield: 8 servings

*This makes a nice dip for entertaining. While it isn't very low in sodium, it's low enough that you can join your guests in having some. Spinach has more natural sodium than most vegetables. I thought I could save some by using fresh instead of frozen, but it doesn't make a significant difference. Most of the sodium comes from the cheeses, and you could reduce them and still have something that tastes good. Also, the amount of sodium in cream cheese and sour cream varies by brand and type, so read the labels carefully.*

**6 ounces (170 g) frozen spinach, thawed and drained**

**2 ounces (55 g) cream cheese**

**½ cup (115 g) sour cream**

**¼ teaspoon garlic powder**

**2 tablespoons (10 g) Parmesan cheese, grated**

**¼ cup (28 g) Monterey Jack cheese, shredded**

Mix all ingredients together in a food processor bowl. Process until smooth. Heat in microwave until warmed through, about 2 minutes. Serve with homemade tortilla chips or low sodium French bread.

**NUTRITIONAL ANALYSIS**

**EACH WITH:** 35 g water; 85 calories (75% from fat, 16% from protein, 9% from carb); 3 g protein; 7 g total fat; 5 g saturated fat; 2 g monounsaturated fat; 0 g polyunsaturated fat; 2 g carb; 1 g fiber; 0 g sugar; 103 mg calcium; 1 mg iron; 95 mg sodium; 100 mg potassium; 2792 IU vitamin A; 1 mg vitamin C; 19 mg cholesterol

# Baked Tortilla Chips

Yield: 1 serving

*Just like you used to get at your favorite Mexican restaurant. I like these sprinkled with a little salt-free taco seasoning. You can also buy unsalted tortilla chips, of course, but once you've had these fresh and warm you won't want those anymore.*

**1 corn tortilla**

**Nonstick vegetable oil spray**

Preheat oven to 350°F (180°C, gas mark 4). Cut tortilla into 6 wedges. Place tortilla pieces on baking sheet. Spray with nonstick vegetable oil spray. Turn over and spray the other side. Bake until crispy and browned on the edges, about 10 minutes.

**NUTRITIONAL ANALYSIS**

**EACH WITH:** 11 g water; 58 calories (10% from fat, 10% from protein, 80% from carb); 1 g protein; 1 g total fat; 0 g saturated fat; 0 g monounsaturated fat; 0 g polyunsaturated fat; 12 g carb; 1 g fiber; 0 g sugar; 45 mg calcium; 0 mg iron; 14 mg sodium; 40 mg potassium; 0 IU vitamin A; 0 mg vitamin C; 0 mg cholesterol

# Mexican Layered Dip

Yield: 8 servings

*Just like at your favorite Mexican restaurant, except this one you're allowed to eat. If you use homemade beans, salsa, and guacamole the final nutritional counts should be about what is listed here. If you used commercial ones, it may be higher.*

½ cup (112.5 g) refried beans

½ cup (112.5 g) guacamole

¼ cup (60 g) sour cream

1 tomato, chopped

¼ cup (30 g) cheddar cheese, shredded

¼ cup (40 g) green onion, chopped

¼ cup (56 g) Dick's Best Salsa (see recipe, page 26)

In a serving dish, layer the ingredients in the order shown.

### NUTRITIONAL ANALYSIS

**EACH WITH:** 36 g water; 65 calories (59% from fat, 14% from protein, 26% from carb); 2 g protein; 4 g total fat; 2 g saturated fat; 2 g monounsaturated fat; 0 g polyunsaturated fat; 4 g carb; 2 g fiber; 1 g sugar; 48 mg calcium; 0 mg iron; 36 mg sodium; 129 mg potassium; 187 IU vitamin A; 4 mg vitamin C; 8 mg cholesterol

# Snack Mix

Yield: 24 servings

*This is very close to the original version of the Chex snack mix. Use unsalted nuts, unsalted pretzels, and low sodium cereal. Chex cereal contains quite a bit of sodium, but you can readily find substitutes like mini shredded wheat and sodium-free versions of oat rings such as Cheerios. A number of good commercial seasoning mixes contain no salt, such as those from Mrs. Dash, Frontier, and Mr. Spice—or use some that you've made.*

6 tablespoons (85 g) unsalted butter

2 tablespoons (30 ml) Worcestershire sauce

1½ teaspoons salt-free seasoning mix

½ teaspoon onion powder

¾ teaspoon garlic powder

½ pound (225 g) pecans, unsalted

½ pound (225 g) dry-roasted peanuts, unsalted

8 ounces (225 g) pretzels, unsalted

3 cups (300 g) mini shredded wheat

3 cups (240 g) low sodium oat cereal

Melt butter. Add seasonings and stir. Combine nuts and pretzels in a large bowl. Pour sauce over and stir to coat. Stir in cereal and mix well. Bake at 275°F (140°C, gas mark 1) for 3 hours, stirring occasionally.

### NUTRITIONAL ANALYSIS

**EACH WITH:** 2 g water; 218 calories (58% from fat, 9% from protein, 33% from carb); 5 g protein; 15 g total fat; 3 g saturated fat; 7 g monounsaturated fat; 4 g polyunsaturated fat; 19 g carb; 3 g fiber; 1 g sugar; 31 mg calcium; 2 mg iron; 39 mg sodium; 164 mg potassium; 158 IU vitamin A; 3 mg vitamin C; 8 mg cholesterol

# Sesame Chicken Wings

Yield: 10 servings

*These can be used as an appetizer or the beginning of a meal. You won't even know they are low sodium.*

20 chicken wings

2 eggs

2 tablespoons (28 ml) skim milk

1½ cups (165 g) Buttermilk Baking Mix (see recipe, page 40)

½ cup (60 g) sesame seeds

2 teaspoons (5 g) paprika

1½ teaspoons dry mustard

2 tablespoons (28 g) unsalted butter, melted

Preheat oven to 425°F (220°C, gas mark 7). Separate chicken wings at joints; discard tips. Spray 2 rectangular 13 x 9-inch (33 x 23-cm) pans with nonstick vegetable oil spray. Beat eggs and milk with fork in bowl. Mix baking mix, sesame seeds, paprika, and mustard in second bowl. Soak chicken in egg mixture in first bowl and then coat with sesame seed mixture in second bowl. Arrange close together in pans. Drizzle butter over chicken. Bake uncovered for 35 to 40 minutes or until brown and crisp.

## NUTRITIONAL ANALYSIS

**EACH WITH:** 30 g water; 87 calories (52% from fat, 45% from protein, 3% from carb); 10 g protein; 5 g total fat; 2 g saturated fat; 1 g monounsaturated fat; 1 g polyunsaturated fat; 1 g carb; 0 g fiber; 0 g sugar; 17 mg calcium; 1 mg iron; 48 mg sodium; 114 mg potassium; 381 IU vitamin A; 0 mg vitamin C; 28 mg cholesterol

# Microwave Potato Chips

Yield: 8 servings

*These potato chips are very easy to make and are healthier for you as they are not cooked in any oils. They can be made plain or with your choice of salt-free herbs and spice mixes. They need to be sliced fairly thin to get crisp, but not paper thin.*

4 medium potatoes

Your choice of spices or herbs, optional

If potatoes are old, peel and slice thin, ⅟₁₆ inch (0.16 cm) in thickness, slicing across the potato. If the potatoes are new or have good skins, do not peel. Just scrub well, then slice them ⅟₁₆ inch (0.16 cm) in thickness, slicing across the potato. Sprinkle with your choice of spices or herbs or just leave them plain. If you have a microwave bacon tray, place the sliced potatoes flat on the tray in a single layer. Cover with a microwavable, round heavy plastic cover. Microwave on high (full power) for 7 to 8 minutes. Cooking time could vary slightly, depending on the wattage of your microwave. You do not have to turn the sliced potatoes over. If you do not have a bacon tray, place between two microwave-safe plates. Plates will be hot by the time potatoes are done. Continue to microwave the remainder of the sliced potatoes as above.

## NUTRITIONAL ANALYSIS

**EACH WITH:** 67 g water; 67 calories (1% from fat, 10% from protein, 89% from carb); 2 g protein; 0 g total fat; 0 g saturated fat; 0 g monounsaturated fat; 0 g polyunsaturated fat; 15 g carb; 1 g fiber; 1 g sugar; 11 mg calcium; 1 mg iron; 4 mg sodium; 354 mg potassium; 1 IU vitamin A; 17 mg vitamin C; 0 mg cholesterol

# Crab-Stuffed Mushrooms

Yield: 6 servings

*This makes a very nice appetizer for entertaining. Like all seafood, crab has a lot of natural sodium and cholesterol, so go easy on it.*

¼ cup (25 g) scallions, minced

2 teaspoons (10 g) unsalted butter

1 can (4 ounces, or 115 g) crabmeat, drained

2 tablespoons (8 g) fresh parsley, minced

1 tablespoon (15 g) horseradish

2 cloves garlic, pressed

¼ teaspoon hot pepper sauce

2½ cups mushroom caps (24), stems removed

Combine scallions and butter in a 2-cup measure. Microwave on high for 2 minutes; stir in crabmeat, parsley, horseradish, garlic, and pepper sauce. Stir well. Place half the mushrooms, stemmed sides up, in a 9-inch (23-cm) pie plate. Fill each mushroom cap with 1 teaspoon crab mixture. Microwave on high for 3 to 4 minutes, turning plate once. Remove mushrooms to serving plate. Repeat with the remaining mushrooms and filling. Let stand for 2 to 3 minutes before serving. To garnish, sprinkle with ground red pepper. Each serving contains 4 mushrooms.

---

**NUTRITIONAL ANALYSIS**

**EACH WITH:** 49 g water; 43 calories (33% from fat, 48% from protein, 19% from carb); 5 g protein; 2 g total fat; 1 g saturated fat; 0 g monounsaturated fat; 0 g polyunsaturated fat; 2 g carb; 1 g fiber; 1 g sugar; 20 mg calcium; 0 mg iron; 83 mg sodium; 198 mg potassium; 209 IU vitamin A; 5 mg vitamin C; 18 mg cholesterol

# Brie Crisps

Yield: 36 servings

*This recipe came along with my recipe software, which says it is from a 1982* Bon Appétit *magazine. The only change I made was to leave out the salt. This is the type of thing that's really impressive for guests and is delightfully low in sodium compared to most appetizers.*

4 ounces (115 g) brie, ripe and room temperature

½ cup (112 g) unsalted butter, room temperature

⅔ cup (73 g) unbleached all-purpose flour

⅛ teaspoon cayenne pepper

Paprika, to taste

Combine cheese and butter in food processor and mix until creamy. Add flour and pepper and mix, using on/off turns, until dough almost forms a ball. Turn dough out onto a large piece of plastic wrap and shape into a loose cylinder 2 inches (5 cm) in diameter. Wrap the dough tightly in plastic and refrigerate for 30 minutes. Roll dough into a smooth cylinder about 1½ inches (4 cm) in diameter and 8 inches (20 cm) long. Rewrap dough in plastic and refrigerate overnight. Preheat oven to 400°F (200°C, gas mark 6). Slice cylinder into ¼-inch-thick (0.64-cm-thick) rounds. Arrange on a baking sheet, spacing about 2 inches (5 cm) apart. Bake until edges are nicely browned, 10 to 12 minutes. Cool on a rack. Sprinkle with paprika and serve.

---

**NUTRITIONAL ANALYSIS**

**EACH WITH:** 2 g water; 42 calories (74% from fat, 9% from protein, 17% from carb); 1 g protein; 3 g total fat; 2 g saturated fat; 1 g monounsaturated fat; 0 g polyunsaturated fat; 2 g carb; 0 g fiber; 0 g sugar; 7 mg calcium; 0 mg iron; 28 mg sodium; 8 mg potassium; 100 IU vitamin A; 0 mg vitamin C; 10 mg cholesterol

# Hummus

Yield: 8 servings

*A traditional Middle Eastern dip. This version that you make at home is much lower in sodium than most of the ones you buy pre-made. You should be able to find dried garbanzos with the other dried beans in most large markets. Feel free to adjust the spices or use different herbs to suit your own taste. If you can't find a low sodium tahini in the store you can make your own using our recipe (see page 43).*

1 cup (100 g) cooked garbanzo beans

3 cloves garlic

3 tablespoons (45 ml) lemon juice

¼ cup (60 ml) water

¼ cup (60 g) tahini

1 teaspoon cumin

½ teaspoon paprika

1 tablespoon (15 ml) olive oil

Place the cooked garbanzo beans in the food processor along with the garlic, lemon juice, and water. Process for about a minute, until smooth. If too thick, add more water. Stir in the tahini and spices, taste, and add more lemon juice/tahini/cumin/paprika as desired. Spread into a shallow bowl; drizzle with olive oil. Serve chilled.

NUTRITIONAL ANALYSIS

**EACH WITH:** 16 g water; 155 calories (41% from fat, 15% from protein, 44% from carb); 6 g protein; 7 g total fat; 1 g saturated fat; 3 g monounsaturated fat; 3 g polyunsaturated fat; 18 g carb; 5 g fiber; 3 g sugar; 63 mg calcium; 2 mg iron; 16 mg sodium; 269 mg potassium; 102 IU vitamin A; 4 mg vitamin C; 0 mg cholesterol

# Bruschetta

Yield: 4 servings

*The simplest form of bruschetta, with just enough garlic to taste and a little olive oil.*

1 loaf low sodium Italian bread

2 cloves garlic

2 tablespoons (30 ml) olive oil, extra virgin

Cut 4 slices from the loaf of bread (no more than ½ inch [1¼ cm] thick) and toast in the oven until light brown, 4 to 5 minutes. Take off the garlic skin and rub the garlic firmly across the face of the toast. Drizzle with just enough olive oil to cover the entire surface of the bread.

NUTRITIONAL ANALYSIS

**EACH WITH:** 12 g water; 143 calories (49% from fat, 8% from protein, 43% from carb); 3 g protein; 8 g total fat; 1 g saturated fat; 5 g monounsaturated fat; 1 g polyunsaturated fat; 15 g carb; 1 g fiber; 0 g sugar; 26 mg calcium; 1 mg iron; 16 mg sodium; 39 mg potassium; 0 IU vitamin A; 0 mg vitamin C; 0 mg cholesterol

# CHAPTER 5

# Breakfast

*I like breakfast. And I like traditional breakfasts with fresh-baked breads, eggs, and sausage. Unfortunately, there aren't many low sodium versions of those things available. So I selfishly started experimenting with breakfast foods. I have to admit that some of the early sausage experiments weren't that good. But eventually they got better. And the food in this chapter would be right at home in any bed and breakfast in the country. So enjoy your morning again.*

# Pancakes

Yield: 3 servings

*This makes 3 large servings of 2 to 3 pancakes each. Don't overmix, or they will become tough.*

1¼ cups (145 g) all-purpose flour

2 tablespoons (26 g) sugar

2 teaspoons (9 g) sodium-free baking powder

1 egg

1 cup (235 ml) milk

1 tablespoon (15 ml) vegetable oil

In a mixing bowl, stir together the dry ingredients. Combine the egg, milk, and oil. Add all at once to the flour mixture. Stir until blended but still slightly lumpy. Pour about ¼ cup of batter onto hot greased griddle for each pancake. Cook until browned on bottom (when bubbles form and then break). Turn and cook on other side until done.

### NUTRITIONAL ANALYSIS

**EACH WITH:** 95 g water; 322 calories (20% from fat, 13% from protein, 67% from carb); 11 g protein; 7 g total fat; 1 g saturated fat; 2 g monounsaturated fat; 3 g polyunsaturated fat; 54 g carb; 1 g fiber; 13 g sugar; 265 mg calcium; 3 mg iron; 65 mg sodium; 546 mg potassium; 261 IU vitamin A; 0 mg vitamin C; 83 mg cholesterol

### TIP

The griddle is hot enough when a drop of water dropped onto it sizzles and breaks up immediately.

# Waffles

Yield: 2 servings

*Waffles are usually fairly high in fat and sodium. This recipe contains less fat than most. The waffles tend to be a little crispier and not as light as the traditional recipe with the beaten egg whites folded in.*

1 cup (110 g) all-purpose flour

1 teaspoon sodium-free baking powder

1 teaspoon sugar

1 egg

¾ cup (175 ml) skim milk

1 tablespoon (14 g) unsalted butter, melted

Mix together dry ingredients. Combine egg, milk, and melted butter. Add to dry ingredients, mixing until just blended. Do not overbeat. Bake according to waffle iron directions.

### NUTRITIONAL ANALYSIS

**EACH WITH:** 113 g water; 369 calories (23% from fat, 15% from protein, 62% from carb); 14 g protein; 9 g total fat; 5 g saturated fat; 3 g monounsaturated fat; 1 g polyunsaturated fat; 56 g carb; 2 g fiber; 2 g sugar; 267 mg calcium; 4 mg iron; 99 mg sodium; 528 mg potassium; 506 IU vitamin A; 1 mg vitamin C; 140 mg cholesterol

# Baked French Toast

Yield: 6 servings

*This makes a great way to use up the remainder of a loaf. It's an easy make-ahead breakfast for a weekend or holiday. You can reduce the fat and calories by leaving off the crumb topping.*

6 slices low sodium bread

3 eggs

3 tablespoons (39 g) sugar

1 teaspoon vanilla extract

2¼ cups (535 ml) skim milk

½ cup (60 g) all-purpose flour

6 tablespoons (90 g) brown sugar

½ teaspoon ground cinnamon, packed

¼ cup (55 g) unsalted butter

1 cup (145 g) blueberries, fresh or frozen

Cut bread into 1-inch (2.5 cm)-thick slices and place in a greased 9 x 13-inch (23 x 33-cm) baking dish. In a medium bowl, lightly beat eggs, sugar, and vanilla. Stir in the milk until well blended. Pour over bread, turning pieces to coat well. Cover and refrigerate overnight. Preheat oven to 375°F (190°C, gas mark 5). In a small bowl, combine the flour, brown sugar, and cinnamon. Cut in butter until mixture resembles coarse crumbs. Turn bread over in baking dish. Scatter blueberries over bread. Sprinkle evenly with crumb mixture. Bake for about 40 minutes until golden brown.

NUTRITIONAL ANALYSIS

**EACH WITH:** 157 g water; 423 calories (27% from fat, 12% from protein, 61% from carb); 12 g protein; 13 g total fat; 6 g saturated fat; 4 g monounsaturated fat; 1 g polyunsaturated fat; 65 g carb; 2 g fiber; 31 g sugar; 216 mg calcium; 3 mg iron; 115 mg sodium; 341 mg potassium; 581 IU vitamin A; 2 mg vitamin C; 145 mg cholesterol

# Banana Fritters

Yield: 4 servings

*A search for a breakfast dish that would use up some overripe bananas was rewarded with this recipe. They are incredibly light and very tasty. Sprinkle with powdered sugar or dip in honey if you don't mind adding a few more calories to the ones they already have.*

1 cup (110 g) all-purpose flour

1 tablespoon (15 g) sugar

1 tablespoon (14 g) sodium-free baking powder

½ cup (120 ml) skim milk

1 egg

1 tablespoon (15 ml) canola oil

1 cup (225 g) banana, chopped

½ teaspoon ground nutmeg

Stir together flour, sugar, and baking powder. Combine the milk, egg, and oil. Add banana and nutmeg. Stir into dry ingredients, stirring until just moistened. Drop by tablespoonfuls into hot oil. Fry for 2 to 3 minutes on a side until golden brown. Drain.

NUTRITIONAL ANALYSIS

**EACH WITH:** 85 g water; 245 calories (20% from fat, 11% from protein, 69% from carb); 7 g protein; 6 g total fat; 1 g saturated fat; 3 g monounsaturated fat; 1 g polyunsaturated fat; 44 g carb; 2 g fiber; 10 g sugar; 222 mg calcium; 2 mg iron; 43 mg sodium; 690 mg potassium; 169 IU vitamin A; 5 mg vitamin C; 62 mg cholesterol

# Cinnamon Pull-Apart Loaf

Yield: 12 servings

*This makes a nice holiday breakfast or just something for one of those lazy Sunday mornings when you want to relax and read the paper.*

4 tablespoons (60 g) sugar, divided

1½ teaspoons ground cinnamon

3½ cups (385 g) Buttermilk Baking Mix (see recipe, page 40)

⅔ cup (157 ml) skim milk

2 tablespoons (28 g) unsalted butter

1 teaspoon vanilla extract

1 egg

½ cup (50 g) powdered sugar

2 tablespoons (30 ml) water

Mix 2 tablespoons sugar and the cinnamon. Place in a resealable plastic bag. Spray a 9 x 5 x 3-inch (23 x 13 x 7.5-cm) loaf pan with nonstick vegetable oil spray. Stir together the baking mix, milk, remaining sugar, butter, vanilla, and egg until it forms a ball. Pinch off 1½-inch (4-cm) pieces. Shake in the cinnamon-sugar mixture until coated and then place in the pan. Bake at 375°F (190°C, gas mark 5) for 25 to 30 minutes or until golden brown. Let stand in pan for 10 minutes before removing. Mix together powdered sugar and water and drizzle over top.

---

**NUTRITIONAL ANALYSIS**

**EACH WITH:** 22 g water; 209 calories (33% from fat, 7% from protein, 60% from carb); 4 g protein; 8 g total fat; 3 g saturated fat; 4 g monounsaturated fat; 1 g polyunsaturated fat; 31 g carb; 1 g fiber; 13 g sugar; 86 mg calcium; 1 mg iron; 21 mg sodium; 88 mg potassium; 113 IU vitamin A; 0 mg vitamin C; 26 mg cholesterol

# Cinnamon Rolls

Yield: 9 servings

*Sometimes you've just gotta have something sinful. If you desire a glaze, mix a few tablespoons of water with enough powdered sugar to make a drizzling consistency.*

FOR DOUGH:

1 cup (235 ml) water

2 tablespoons (28 ml) vegetable oil

1 egg

3 cups (330 g) bread flour

¼ cup (50 g) sugar

3 teaspoons (12 g) yeast

FOR FILLING:

⅓ cup (67 g) sugar

2 teaspoons (5 g) ground cinnamon

2 tablespoons (28 g) unsalted butter, softened

Place dough ingredients in bread machine in the order specified by manufacturer. Process on dough cycle. Remove dough and press out to a 9 x 18-inch (23 x 46-cm) rectangle on a lightly floured board. Mix together cinnamon and sugar. Spread dough with softened butter, then sprinkle with cinnamon-sugar mixture. Roll up tightly, beginning on the 9-inch (23-cm) side. Slice into 9 slices. Place cut side down in a greased 9 x 9-inch (23 x 23-cm) baking pan. Cover and let rise until doubled, 30 to 45 minutes. Bake at 375°F (190°C, gas mark 5) until golden, 25 to 30 minutes.

---

**NUTRITIONAL ANALYSIS**

**EACH WITH:** 38 g water; 280 calories (23% from fat, 10% from protein, 67% from carb); 7 g protein; 7 g total fat; 2 g saturated fat; 2 g monounsaturated fat; 2 g polyunsaturated fat; 47 g carb; 2 g fiber; 13 g sugar; 19 mg calcium; 3 mg iron; 12 mg sodium; 85 mg potassium; 112 IU vitamin A; 0 mg vitamin C; 34 mg cholesterol

# Honey-Topped Coffee Cake

Yield: 8 servings

*A tropical coffee cake with a pineapple/coconut/honey topping. If your spice rack doesn't contain any mace, go get some. It adds a hard-to-describe taste but gives a very nice flavor to this breakfast treat.*

1½ cups (165 g) all-purpose flour

½ cup (100 g) sugar

2 teaspoons (9 g) sodium-free baking powder

½ teaspoon mace

1 can (8¾ ounces, or 255 g) pineapple, crushed

1 egg

¼ cup (60 ml) vegetable oil

⅓ cup (115 g) honey

½ cup (57 g) granola

¼ cup (18 g) coconut

Stir together dry ingredients. Drain pineapple, reserving syrup. Add water to syrup if necessary to make ½ cup. Combine syrup, egg, and oil. Add to flour mixture, stirring until smooth. Pour into 9 x 1½-inch (23 x 4-cm) round baking pan sprayed with nonstick vegetable oil spray. Combine honey, pineapple, granola, and coconut. Spread over batter. Bake at 400°F (200°C, gas mark 6) until done, about 25 minutes.

### NUTRITIONAL ANALYSIS

**EACH WITH:** 38 g water; 314 calories (29% from fat, 6% from protein, 65% from carb); 5 g protein; 10 g total fat; 2 g saturated fat; 3 g monounsaturated fat; 5 g polyunsaturated fat; 52 g carb; 2 g fiber; 30 g sugar; 73 mg calcium; 2 mg iron; 15 mg sodium; 250 mg potassium; 49 IU vitamin A; 3 mg vitamin C; 31 mg cholesterol

# Apple Strata

Yield: 4 servings

*This has become a traditional Christmas morning breakfast. The original recipe called for ham, but no one seems to miss it. You could use any low sodium leftover bread, but I like honey wheat. If you can't find canned apples, you can use apple pie filling, although the result will be sweeter.*

3 cups low sodium bread, cubed

1 can (15 ounces, or 455 g) apples

3 ounces (85 g) Swiss cheese, shredded

4 eggs

¼ cup (60 ml) skim milk

Cube bread and place in a 9-inch-square (23-cm-square) pan sprayed with nonstick vegetable oil spray. Spoon apples over bread. Sprinkle with cheese. Combine eggs and milk and pour over bread, apples, and cheese. Cover with plastic wrap and refrigerate overnight. Heat oven to 350°F (180°C, gas mark 4). Bake uncovered for 40 to 45 minutes or until top is lightly browned and center is set.

### NUTRITIONAL ANALYSIS

**EACH WITH:** 106 g water; 277 calories (42% from fat, 24% from protein, 33% from carb); 17 g protein; 13 g total fat; 6 g saturated fat; 4 g monounsaturated fat; 1 g polyunsaturated fat; 23 g carb; 1 g fiber; 5 g sugar; 295 mg calcium; 2 mg iron; 102 mg sodium; 198 mg potassium; 500 IU vitamin A; 1 mg vitamin C; 266 mg cholesterol

# Sausage

Yield: 8 servings

*It's impossible to find low sodium sausage, so I've learned to make my own. You can buy ground pork in most large supermarkets, but if you have a grinder you can make a much lower-fat version by trimming leaner cuts of pork and grinding them yourself.*

1 pound (455 g) pork, ground

¼ teaspoon black pepper

¼ teaspoon white pepper

¾ teaspoon dried sage

¼ teaspoon mace

½ teaspoon garlic powder

¼ teaspoon onion powder

¼ teaspoon ground allspice

Combine all ingredients, mixing well. Fry, grill, or cook on a greased baking sheet in a 325°F (170°C, gas mark 3) oven until done.

**NUTRITIONAL ANALYSIS**

**EACH WITH:** 38 g water; 121 calories (60% from fat, 38% from protein, 1% from carb); 11 g protein; 8 g total fat; 3 g saturated fat; 4 g monounsaturated fat; 1 g polyunsaturated fat; 0 g carb; 0 g fiber; 0 g sugar; 5 mg calcium; 0 mg iron; 24 mg sodium; 223 mg potassium; 8 IU vitamin A; 0 mg vitamin C; 34 mg cholesterol

# Sausage Gravy

Yield: 4 servings

*If you make your own sausage, then you can still have sausage gravy and biscuits for breakfast. It's great for a cold winter morning, but I have to confess to liking it just about any time. It can also be served over mashed potatoes.*

½ pound (225 g) Sausage (see recipe at left)

3 tablespoons (24 g) all-purpose flour

1 cup (235 ml) skim milk

¼ teaspoon black pepper

Remove sausage with a slotted spoon; set aside. Remove all but 2 tablespoons (28 ml) of grease from the skillet. Over medium heat, stir 3 tablespoons (24 g) of flour into the grease. Stir constantly until browned, about 5 minutes. Stirring constantly, pour in milk. Season with pepper. Continue stirring until the gravy is thick. Add sausage back into the gravy. Serve over split biscuits, grits, or mashed potatoes, or pour into a bowl or gravy boat and serve on the side.

**NUTRITIONAL ANALYSIS**

**EACH WITH:** 88 g water; 219 calories (64% from fat, 22% from protein, 15% from carb); 12 g protein; 15 g total fat; 5 g saturated fat; 7 g monounsaturated fat; 2 g polyunsaturated fat; 8 g carb; 0 g fiber; 0 g sugar; 95 mg calcium; 1 mg iron; 77 mg sodium; 260 mg potassium; 168 IU vitamin A; 1 mg vitamin C; 42 mg cholesterol

# Breakfast Burritos

Yield: 6 servings

*For those days when you want a little something different for breakfast. You could make your own tortillas or use corn ones, which typically don't contain added salt, and make breakfast enchiladas.*

1 medium potato

½ pound (225 g) Sausage (see recipe, page 58)

1 small onion, chopped

1 teaspoon chili powder

¼ teaspoon cayenne pepper

2 eggs

6 flour tortillas

1 cup (110 g) Swiss cheese, shredded

¼ cup (45 g) tomato, chopped

2 tablespoons (30 g) sour cream

¼ cup (56 g) Dick's Best Salsa (see page 26)

Cook potato in boiling water for 35 minutes until tender. When cool, peel and cut into cubes. Brown sausage in frying pan and add onion, chili powder, and cayenne pepper. Cook for 10 minutes. Drain and discard fat. Add cubed, cooked potato. Beat eggs and add to pan. Stir until eggs are set. Spoon mixture into center of warmed tortilla, top with shredded cheese, and roll up tortilla to enclose mixture. For an authentic Mexican touch, serve topped with tomato, sour cream, and salsa.

**NUTRITIONAL ANALYSIS**

**EACH WITH:** 132 g water; 443 calories (46% from fat, 18% from protein, 36% from carb); 19 g protein; 22 g total fat; 9 g saturated fat; 9 g monounsaturated fat; 2 g polyunsaturated fat; 40 g carb; 3 g fiber; 2 g sugar; 264 mg calcium; 3 mg iron; 306 mg sodium; 443 mg potassium; 616 IU vitamin A; 8 mg vitamin C; 131 mg cholesterol

# Breakfast Tacos

Yield: 4 servings

*If the breakfast burritos are a little high in sodium for you, here's an alternative. Corn tortillas and taco shells are usually made without the added salt that's in flour tortillas. And here's an extra tip that you can use for your regular tacos too ... make them breakproof by putting the filling in before you heat them. The extra moisture will make them just soft enough not to fall in half.*

4 eggs

¼ cup (56 g) Dick's Best Salsa (see page 26)

¼ cup (28 g) Swiss cheese, shredded

8 taco shells

Scramble eggs, stirring in salsa and cheese when they are almost set. Divide into taco shells, sitting them upright in an 8 x 8-inch (20 x 20-cm) baking dish. Microwave for 1 minute or heat at 350°F (180°C, gas mark 4) for 5 minutes.

**NUTRITIONAL ANALYSIS**

**EACH WITH:** 63 g water; 243 calories (51% from fat, 19% from protein, 30% from carb); 12 g protein; 14 g total fat; 4 g saturated fat; 5 g monounsaturated fat; 3 g polyunsaturated fat; 18 g carb; 2 g fiber; 1 g sugar; 142 mg calcium; 2 mg iron; 100 mg sodium; 165 mg potassium; 459 IU vitamin A; 2 mg vitamin C; 253 mg cholesterol

# Huevos Rancheros

Yield: 4 servings

*"Ranch-style eggs" in Spanish, this is a typical Mexican breakfast meal. You can make a single serving for yourself using 1 tortilla and 1 egg and an ovenproof bowl.*

2 tablespoons (30 ml) vegetable oil

4 corn tortillas

¼ cup (40 g) onion, chopped

2 cups (360 g) tomatoes, chopped

2 ounces (55 g) chopped chile peppers

4 eggs

½ cup (55 g) Swiss cheese, shredded

In a small skillet, heat the oil. Cook the tortillas in oil for about 10 seconds on a side, until limp. Line an 8 x 8-inch (20 x 20-cm) baking dish with tortillas. In the same skillet, cook the onion until soft. Stir in the tomatoes and chile peppers. Simmer for about 10 minutes. Spoon over the tortillas. Carefully break the eggs into the skillet. When the whites are set, add a tablespoon of water, cover, and cook until the yolks are almost at desired doneness. Add the eggs over the sauce in a baking dish. Sprinkle with cheese. Place under broiler just until cheese melts.

**NUTRITIONAL ANALYSIS**

**EACH WITH:** 153 g water; 289 calories (55% from fat, 20% from protein, 25% from carb); 14 g protein; 18 g total fat; 6 g saturated fat; 5 g monounsaturated fat; 5 g polyunsaturated fat; 18 g carb; 3 g fiber; 4 g sugar; 247 mg calcium; 2 mg iron; 102 mg sodium; 375 mg potassium; 1205 IU vitamin A; 44 mg vitamin C; 261 mg cholesterol

# Soft Granola Bars

Yield: 27 servings

*Granola bars don't have to contain sodium. You could add unsalted nuts to this if you wanted or substitute chocolate chips or other dried fruit for the raisins.*

3 cups (240 g) quick-cooking oats

½ cup (115 g) brown sugar

¼ cup (28 g) wheat germ

½ cup (112 g) unsalted butter

¼ cup (60 ml) corn syrup

¼ cup (85 g) honey

½ cup (82.5 g) raisins

½ cup (35 g) sweetened coconut

Combine the oats, sugar, and wheat germ. Cut in the butter until the mixture is crumbly. Stir in the corn syrup and honey. Add the raisins and coconut. Press into a greased 9-inch (23-cm) square pan. Bake at 350°F (180°C, gas mark 4) for 20 to 25 minutes. Let cool for 10 minutes, then cut into bars.

**NUTRITIONAL ANALYSIS**

**EACH WITH:** 4 g water; 153 calories (30% from fat, 8% from protein, 61% from carb); 3 g protein; 5 g total fat; 3 g saturated fat; 1 g monounsaturated fat; 1 g polyunsaturated fat; 24 g carb; 2 g fiber; 11 g sugar; 16 mg calcium; 1 mg iron; 11 mg sodium; 129 mg potassium; 105 IU vitamin A; 0 mg vitamin C; 9 mg cholesterol

# Power Bars

Yield: 12 servings

*These contain a little more nutrition than the granola bars and are equally good for a breakfast on the run.*

- 1 cup (80 g) quick-cooking oats
- ½ cup (75 g) whole wheat flour
- ½ cup (57 g) Grape-Nuts cereal, or other nugget-type cereal
- ½ teaspoon ground cinnamon
- 1 egg
- ¼ cup (60 g) applesauce
- ¼ cup (85 g) honey
- 3 tablespoons (45 g) brown sugar
- 2 tablespoons (30 ml) vegetable oil
- ¼ cup (56 g) sunflower seeds, unsalted
- ¼ cup (35 g) walnuts, chopped
- 7 ounces (198 g) dried fruit

Preheat oven to 325°F (170°C, gas mark 3). Line a 9-inch (23-cm) square baking pan with aluminum foil. Spray the foil with cooking spray. In a large bowl, stir together the oats, flour, cereal, and cinnamon. Add the egg, applesauce, honey, brown sugar, and oil. Mix well. Stir in the sunflower seeds, walnuts, and dried fruit. Spread mixture evenly in the prepared pan. Bake for 30 minutes, or until firm and lightly browned around the edges. Let cool. Use the foil to lift from the pan. Cut into bars and store in the refrigerator.

**NUTRITIONAL ANALYSIS**

**EACH WITH:** 16 g water; 223 calories (26% from fat, 10% from protein, 65% from carb); 6 g protein; 7 g total fat; 1 g saturated fat; 2 g monounsaturated fat; 4 g polyunsaturated fat; 38 g carb; 4 g fiber; 10 g sugar; 27 mg calcium; 3 mg iron; 43 mg sodium; 285 mg potassium; 493 IU vitamin A; 1 mg vitamin C; 20 mg cholesterol

# Breakfast Mix

Yield: 16 servings

*You may have seen the ads for Chex Breakfast Mix, a great idea for people needing breakfast on the run. Depending on the flavor, they run about 160 to 180 mg of sodium per bag. I thought we could do better by being more careful with the cereal we pick. The serving size is ½ cup (57 g), but even if you eat more, it shouldn't hurt you too badly.*

- 2 cups (200 g) bite-size frosted shredded wheat cereal
- 2 cups (200 g) Kellogg's Cracklin' Oat Bran or other bite-size low sodium cereal
- ½ cup (75 g) dry-roasted peanuts
- ½ cup (82.5 g) raisins
- 2 cups unsalted pretzels
- 3 tablespoons (60 g) honey
- 3 tablespoons (45 ml) corn syrup
- 1 tablespoon (14 g) unsalted butter
- 1 teaspoon ground cinnamon
- ¼ teaspoon ground nutmeg

Mix cereal, nuts, raisins, and pretzels in a large bowl. Combine the honey, corn syrup, butter, and spices. Microwave until boiling. Pour over cereal mixture, stirring to coat. Place in an ungreased 9 x 13-inch (23 x 33-cm) pan. Bake for 20 minutes at 325°F (170°C, gas mark 3), stirring after 10 minutes. Turn out onto waxed paper. Separate and cool. Store in an airtight container.

**NUTRITIONAL ANALYSIS**

**EACH WITH:** 3 g water; 114 calories (24% from fat, 8% from protein, 68% from carb); 3 g protein; 3 g total fat; 1 g saturated fat; 1 g monounsaturated fat; 1 g polyunsaturated fat; 21 g carb; 2 g fiber; 12 g sugar; 12 mg calcium; 5 mg iron; 41 mg sodium; 116 mg potassium; 153 IU vitamin A; 11 mg vitamin C; 2 mg cholesterol

CHAPTER 6

# Chicken and Turkey

---

*Chicken and turkey are great deals nutritionally, lean and full of protein. However, there are a few things to be aware of. In the United States, much of the chicken and turkey is "enhanced" with injections of a broth solution that is high in sodium, raising the level per serving from well under 100 mg to more than 300 mg. This is done to keep the poultry more juicy (and in some people's opinion to sell you salty water at the same price as good meat). In my area there are a few stores that go against this trend and still sell unenhanced meat. However, you need to look for them and be aware of what you are buying.*

# Beer Can Chicken

Yield: 8 servings

*This recipe has been around a while. It makes a nice tender, juicy bird, either on the grill or in the oven. For a nonalcoholic chicken, substitute ginger ale. You should use the indirect method, which means that you set up your fire so that it is hottest away from the food. On a charcoal grill, arrange it in two piles at opposite sides of the grill. Place a foil drip pan in the center of the grill between the mounds of embers. On a gas grill, if it has two burners, light one side on high and cook the chicken on the other.*

1 chicken, 4 to 6 pounds (1¾ to 2¾ kg)

3 tablespoons Memphis Rub
(see recipe, page 18)

1 can (12 ounces) beer

3 cloves garlic

Remove and discard the fat from inside the body cavities of the chicken. Remove the package of giblets and set aside for another use. Rinse the chicken, inside and out, under cold running water; then drain and blot dry, inside and out, with paper towels. Sprinkle 1 tablespoon of the rub inside the body and neck cavities; then rub the rest all over the skin of the bird. If you wish, rub another half-tablespoon of the mixture between the flesh and the skin. Cover and refrigerate the chicken while you preheat the grill.

Pop the tab on the beer can. Using a "church key" type of can opener, punch 6 or 7 holes in the top of the can. Pour out the top inch (2.5 cm) of beer; drop the peeled garlic cloves into the holes in the can. Holding the chicken upright (wings at top, legs at bottom) with the opening of the body cavity down, insert the beer can into the lower cavity. Oil the grill grate. Stand the chicken up in the center of the hot grate, over the drip pan. Spread out the legs to form a sort of tripod, to support the bird. Cover the grill and cook the chicken until fall-off-the-bone tender, about an hour, depending on size. Use a thermometer to check for doneness. The internal temperature should be 180°F (82°C). Using tongs, lift the bird to a cutting board or platter, holding a metal spatula underneath the beer can for support.

## NUTRITIONAL ANALYSIS

**EACH WITH:** 25 g water; 81 calories (66% from fat, 32% from protein, 2% from carb); 6 g protein; 6 g total fat; 2 g saturated fat; 2 g monounsaturated fat; 1 g polyunsaturated fat; 0 g carb; 0 g fiber; 0 g sugar; 6 mg calcium; 0 mg iron; 25 mg sodium; 76 mg potassium; 48 IU vitamin A; 0 mg vitamin C; 27 mg cholesterol

# Sticky Chicken

Yield: 8 servings

*This unusual recipe is a variation of one posted in the Busy Cooks forum on About. com. The spices give it a flavor similar to the carryout rotisserie chickens. The slow-cooking method leaves the meat very juicy and gives it time to absorb more of the flavor.*

1 teaspoon cayenne pepper

1 teaspoon onion powder

1 teaspoon dried thyme

1 teaspoon white pepper

½ teaspoon black pepper

½ teaspoon garlic powder

½ teaspoon chili powder

1 chicken, the larger the better

Combine the spices in a small bowl. Remove the giblets and neck from the chicken. Wash and dry the chicken inside and out. Rub the spices into the chicken inside and out, making sure to rub deep into the skin. Place the chicken in a sealed zip-top plastic bag and allow to sit in the refrigerator overnight. When ready to roast, remove the chicken from the bag and place in a roasting pan. Roast at 250°F (120°C, gas mark ½) for 5 hours. After the first hour, baste the chicken with the pan juices every half hour. At the end of roasting, remove the chicken from the oven and let stand 10 minutes before carving.

## NUTRITIONAL ANALYSIS

**EACH WITH:** 19 g water; 34 calories (23% from fat, 66% from protein, 11% from carb); 5 g protein; 1 g total fat; 0 g saturated fat; 0 g monounsaturated fat; 0 g polyunsaturated fat; 1 g carb; 0 g fiber; 0 g sugar; 9 mg calcium; 1 mg iron; 20 mg sodium; 71 mg potassium; 156 IU vitamin A; 1 mg vitamin C; 17 mg cholesterol

# Tandoori Chicken

Yield: 8 servings

*A slightly tangy, not overly hot version of this Indian classic. If you like hotter food, you can add more cayenne.*

1 cup (230 g) plain low-fat yogurt

½ teaspoon cardamom

½ teaspoon cumin

½ teaspoon turmeric

⅛ teaspoon cayenne pepper

1 teaspoon bay leaf, crushed

½ teaspoon garlic powder

¾ teaspoon ground ginger

¼ cup (40 g) minced onion

¼ cup (60 ml) lime juice

¼ teaspoon black pepper

1 teaspoon ground cinnamon

1 teaspoon coriander

8 chicken thighs

Combine yogurt with all other spices, mixing well. Prick chicken with a fork. In a plastic food bag or glass pan large enough to hold the chicken, cover the chicken with yogurt marinade, making sure all surfaces of the chicken are coated. Cover and refrigerate for a minimum of 3 hours, but overnight is best. Turn at least once while marinating. Grill over medium coals until done or place chicken in a greased roasting pan with marinade and cook at 375°F (190°C, gas mark 5) for 45 minutes to 1 hour or until chicken is tender.

## NUTRITIONAL ANALYSIS

**EACH WITH:** 64 g water; 82 calories (24% from fat, 49% from protein, 28% from carb); 10 g protein; 2 g total fat; 1 g saturated fat; 1 g monounsaturated fat; 0 g polyunsaturated fat; 6 g carb; 1 g fiber; 3 g sugar; 75 mg calcium; 1 mg iron; 58 mg sodium; 232 mg potassium; 70 IU vitamin A; 5 mg vitamin C; 36 mg cholesterol

# Fried Chicken

Yield: 8 servings

*This is a bit of an effort, which is probably a good thing, because it isn't the healthiest thing you can eat, fat-wise. It also is not particularly cheap, no matter how good a sale the chicken is on, but it's still a lot cheaper than a bucket from the local carryout, a whole lot more healthy, and to my mind much better tasting. It's spicy, but not overly so. Don't be afraid of the amount of cayenne in it; you end up throwing out a fair portion of both the marinade and the coating. Because of this, the nutritional analysis is going to show a bit higher figures than what you actually end up eating. An electric fryer or electric frying pan works best for this so you can easily control the temperature and get it crispy without burning. This recipe was developed from one on Epicurious.com. Most of the sodium is in the Dijon mustard and the buttermilk, so get the lowest-sodium variety you can or make your own mustard.*

1 chicken, cut into pieces, 3 to 4 pounds (1½ to 1¾ kg)

FOR MARINADE:

2 cups (475 ml) buttermilk

¼ cup (60 g) Dijon mustard

1 tablespoon (9 g) onion powder

1 teaspoon dry mustard

1 teaspoon cayenne pepper

1 teaspoon black pepper

FOR COATING:

3 cups (330 g) all-purpose flour

1 tablespoon (14 g) sodium-free baking powder

1 tablespoon (9 g) garlic powder

1 tablespoon (9 g) onion powder

1 tablespoon (9 g) dry mustard

1 tablespoon cayenne pepper

1½ teaspoons black pepper

Cut chicken into pieces. In a 1-gallon resealable plastic bag, combine marinade ingredients. Add chicken pieces. Seal bag and turn to coat chicken evenly. Refrigerate at least overnight and up to 2 days, turning occasionally. Whisk together coating ingredients in a 9 x 13-inch (23 x 33-cm) baking dish. Add chicken pieces to dish, allowing as much marinade to stay on the chicken as you can. Turn to coat evenly and thickly. Let stand in coating mix 1 to 2 hours, turning occasionally. Chicken will continue to absorb flour. The idea is to get a thick coating completely covering the chicken to seal in the juices when it's fried. Heat oil to a depth of at least 1½ inches (4 cm) in a deep fryer or heavy frying pan. Heat to 350°F (180°C, gas mark 4). Add 4 pieces of chicken. Reduce heat to 300°F (150°C, gas mark 2). Fry for 5 minutes. Turn carefully to avoid breaking coating. Fry until done through, about 15 minutes depending on size of pieces. Reheat oil to 350°F (180°C, gas mark 4) and fry the remaining 4 pieces the same way. Serve hot or cold.

## NUTRITIONAL ANALYSIS

**EACH WITH:** 88 g water; 247 calories (8% from fat, 21% from protein, 70% from carb); 13 g protein; 2 g total fat; 1 g saturated fat; 1 g monounsaturated fat; 1 g polyunsaturated fat; 43 g carb; 2 g fiber; 4 g sugar; 182 mg calcium; 3 mg iron; 91 mg sodium; 458 mg potassium; 412 IU vitamin A; 3 mg vitamin C; 20 mg cholesterol

# Honey Chicken

Yield: 4 servings

*The stir-frying and ingredients give this dish an Asian feel, although it doesn't use the typical seasonings. It's good over rice, and I would think it would go well with pasta too.*

2½ tablespoons (35 ml) vegetable oil, divided

1 pound (455 g) sliced boneless chicken breast

1 egg

⅓ cup (43 g) cornstarch

2 onions, sliced

1 green bell pepper, sliced

6 ounces (170 g) snow peas

¼ cup (85 g) honey

2 tablespoons (16 g) sliced almonds

Heat 1½ (25 ml) tablespoons of the oil in a wok. Dip half the chicken in the egg and dust with cornstarch. Stir-fry until just cooked, 4 to 5 minutes. Remove and repeat with remaining chicken. Remove; add the rest of the oil to the wok. Stir-fry the onion until it begins to soften. Add the pepper and snow peas and stir-fry until crisp cooked, about 4 minutes. Add the honey and toss the vegetables in it until well coated. Add the chicken and toss until coated and heated through. Sprinkle the almonds over the top.

**NUTRITIONAL ANALYSIS**

**EACH WITH:** 216 g water; 466 calories (32% from fat, 34% from protein, 34% from carb); 40 g protein; 17 g total fat; 3 g saturated fat; 6 g monounsaturated fat; 7 g polyunsaturated fat; 39 g carb; 3 g fiber; 23 g sugar; 71 mg calcium; 3 mg iron 112 mg sodium; 590 mg potassium; 695 IU vitamin A; 59 mg vitamin C; 158 mg cholesterol

# Blackened Chicken

Yield: 4 servings

*Nice Cajun flavor off the grill.*

4 chicken thighs

2 tablespoons (28 g) unsalted butter, melted

5 teaspoons (12.5 g) Cajun Blackening Spice Mix (see recipe, page 20)

Trim excess fat from the chicken. Cut slashes through the skin and ½ inch (1¼ cm) deep to allow spices to penetrate the meat. Brush the thighs with the melted butter, then rub the spices in. Cook on a medium grill for about 25 minutes.

**NUTRITIONAL ANALYSIS**

**EACH WITH:** 32 g water; 100 calories (67% from fat, 33% from protein, 0% from carb); 8 g protein; 7 g total fat; 4 g saturated fat; 2 g monounsaturated fat; 1 g polyunsaturated fat; 0 g carb; 0 g fiber; 0 g sugar; 6 mg calcium; 0 mg iron; 36 mg sodium; 96 mg potassium; 204 IU vitamin A; 0 mg vitamin C; 49 mg cholesterol

# Orange Burgundy Chicken

Yield: 4 servings

*My daughter made this one evening while I was busy taking advantage of a little sunshine to get some yard work done. It's definitely something we'll have again.*

¼ cup (75 g) orange marmalade

½ tablespoon cornstarch

¼ cup (60 ml) burgundy wine

4 boneless chicken breasts

In a small saucepan, combine the first 3 ingredients. Cook and stir until thickened and bubbly. Grill chicken breasts until done, about 15 minutes on a charcoal or gas grill (may also be baked in the oven). Brush sauce over chicken during last 5 minutes of cooking. Serve remaining sauce over chicken.

### NUTRITIONAL ANALYSIS

**EACH WITH:** 54 g water; 147 calories (12% from fat, 47% from protein, 40% from carb); 16 g protein; 2 g total fat; 1 g saturated fat; 1 g monounsaturated fat; 0 g polyunsaturated fat; 14 g carb; 0 g fiber; 12 g sugar; 17 mg calcium; 1 mg iron; 50 mg sodium; 157 mg potassium; 23 IU vitamin A; 1 mg vitamin C; 44 mg cholesterol

# Buffalo Chicken Thighs

Yield: 6 servings

*A main-dish version of Buffalo chicken, using grilled thighs instead.*

5 chicken thighs, skinned

2 tablespoons (28 g) unsalted butter

3 tablespoons hot pepper sauce

2 tablespoons (30 ml) white vinegar

Grill thighs over medium coals, turning frequently until done, about 30 minutes. Melt butter in a small saucepan; add the hot pepper sauce and white vinegar. Place the chicken in a large resealable plastic bag. Pour the mixture over the chicken, seal, and shake to coat. Remove, allowing extra sauce to drain.

### NUTRITIONAL ANALYSIS

**EACH WITH:** 38 g water; 76 calories (62% from fat, 36 % from protein, 2% from carb); 7 g protein; 5 g total fat; 3 g saturated fat; 1 g monounsaturated fat; 1 g polyunsaturated fat; 0 g carb; 0 g fiber; 0 g sugar; 6 mg calcium; 0 mg iron; 75 mg sodium; 94 mg potassium; 256 IU vitamin A; 0 mg vitamin C; 39 mg cholesterol

# Polynesian Chicken

Yield: 4 servings

*This was kind of a throw-together one night when we didn't know what to have for dinner. We happened to have chicken thighs on hand, but you could use whatever pieces you prefer. The flavor is like a mild sweet-and-sour chicken.*

- 8 ounces (225 g) pineapple chunks
- ¼ cup (85 g) honey
- ¼ cup (60 ml) red wine vinegar
- 4 chicken thighs
- ½ cup (60 g) red bell pepper, chopped
- ½ cup (80 g) onion, coarsely chopped

Drain pineapple, reserving juice. Combine juice, honey, and vinegar. Place chicken in an 8 x 13-inch (20 x 33-cm) baking pan. Sprinkle pineapple and vegetables over top. Pour juice mixture over. Bake at 350°F (180°C, gas mark 4) until chicken is done, about 45 minutes.

---

**NUTRITIONAL ANALYSIS**

**EACH WITH:** 126 g water; 144 calories (10% from fat, 23% from protein, 67% from carb); 9 g protein; 2 g total fat; 0 g saturated fat; 1 g monounsaturated fat; 0 g polyunsaturated fat; 26 g carb; 1 g fiber; 24 g sugar; 20 mg calcium; 1 mg iron; 38 mg sodium; 241 mg potassium; 337 IU vitamin A; 23 mg vitamin C; 34 mg cholesterol

# Southwestern Chicken Breasts

Yield: 4 servings

*The fat content listed is probably a little high since it assumes all the marinade is absorbed, but you will have some left to throw away.*

- 4 boneless skinless chicken breast halves
- 4 ounces (115 g) Swiss cheese

FOR MARINADE:
- ⅓ cup (80 ml) vegetable oil
- ⅓ cup (80 ml) lime juice
- 2 tablespoons (18 g) green chiles, chopped
- ¼ teaspoon garlic powder

In a 9-inch (23-cm) square glass baking pan stir together all of the marinade ingredients. Add chicken breasts and marinate, turning once, in the refrigerator, for at least 45 minutes. Remove the chicken from the marinade. Drain. Grill or sauté chicken over medium heat for 7 minutes. Turn. Continue cooking until done, 6 to 8 minutes longer. Top each chicken breast with a slice of cheese. Continue cooking until cheese begins to melt. Serve with salsa.

---

**NUTRITIONAL ANALYSIS**

**EACH WITH:** 76 g water; 246 calories (70% from fat, 27% from protein, 4% from carb); 17 g protein; 19 g total fat; 3 g saturated fat; 5 g monounsaturated fat; 11 g polyunsaturated fat; 2 g carb; 0 g fiber; 0 g sugar; 11 mg calcium; 1 mg iron; 64 mg sodium; 210 mg potassium; 30 IU vitamin A; 8 mg vitamin C; 41 mg cholesterol

---

**TIP**

These make a good meal with some Spanish rice.

## Sun-Dried Tomato Coated Chicken

Yield: 2 servings

*Add a little extra flavor to a coated chicken breast with sun-dried tomatoes. This plus roasted Italian-style vegetables was one of the meals we created when we decided to "get back to less-fattening foods."*

2 boneless chicken breasts

½ cup (60 g) low sodium bread crumbs

¼ cup (27.5 g) sun-dried tomatoes in oil

1 clove garlic, minced

1 egg

2 tablespoons (30 ml) olive oil

Split chicken breasts in half to make two thin cutlets (or pound them flat, but that always seemed like wasted effort to me). Combine bread crumbs, tomatoes, and garlic in food processor. Process until well blended. Dip chicken in beaten eggs and then in crumb mixture to coat thoroughly. Heat oil in an ovenproof skillet. Brown chicken about 2 minutes on each side, until just golden brown. Transfer skillet to a preheated 400°F (200°C, gas mark 6) oven and cook until chicken is cooked through, about 10 minutes.

**NUTRITIONAL ANALYSIS**

**EACH WITH:** 66 g water; 386 calories (51% from fat, 25% from protein, 24% from carb); 24 g protein; 22 g total fat; 4 g saturated fat; 13 g monounsaturated fat; 3 g polyunsaturated fat; 23 g carb; 2 g fiber; 2 g sugar; 82 mg calcium; 3 mg iron; 126 mg sodium; 446 mg potassium; 328 IU vitamin A; 14 mg vitamin C; 167 mg cholesterol

## Chicken Nuggets

Yield: 4 servings

*A do-it-yourself version of the unhealthy fast food. This has proven to be a favorite with both young children and teenagers. My own children said they tasted better than the restaurant ones (well, actually two out of three did).*

1 pound (455 g) boneless chicken breast

½ cup (19 g) cornflakes, crushed

2 tablespoons nonfat dry milk

1 tablespoon (0.4 g) dried parsley

1 tablespoon (7 g) paprika

1 teaspoon onion powder

¼ teaspoon garlic powder

½ teaspoon poultry seasoning

1 egg, beaten

Cut chicken into nugget-size pieces. Mix together cornflakes, dry milk, and spices in a resealable plastic bag. Dip chicken pieces in egg, then place in bag. Shake to coat evenly. Place on baking sheet sprayed with nonstick vegetable oil spray. Bake at 350°F (180°C, gas mark 4) until chicken is done and coating is crispy, about 20 minutes.

**NUTRITIONAL ANALYSIS**

**EACH WITH:** 97 g water; 174 calories (17% from fat, 70% from protein, 13% from carb); 29 g protein; 3 g total fat; 1 g saturated fat; 1 g monounsaturated fat; 1 g polyunsaturated fat; 6 g carb; 1 g fiber; 2 g sugar; 55 mg calcium; 2 mg iron; 137 mg sodium; 402 mg potassium; 1148 IU vitamin A; 4 mg vitamin C; 127 mg cholesterol

# Chicken Kabobs

Yield: 4 servings

*A little taste of the islands ... mildly spicy, but flavorful.*

- 18 ounces (504 g) pineapple chunks
- 1 teaspoon cumin
- 1 teaspoon coriander
- ⅛ teaspoon garlic powder
- 1 tablespoon (7.5 g) chili powder
- 1 teaspoon cilantro
- 2 tablespoons (30 g) plain low-fat yogurt
- 10 ounces (280 g) boneless skinless chicken breast
- 1 red bell pepper
- 1 onion
- 8 cherry tomatoes

Drain pineapple, reserving juice. In a large bowl, blend together spices and yogurt. Add juice from pineapple and stir to mix. Cut the chicken into cubes and add to the mixture. Cover and refrigerate for 1 to 1½ hours. Cut pepper and onion into cubes. Arrange chicken, pineapple, and vegetables on skewers. Grill over medium heat about 10 minutes, turning and basting with remaining marinade frequently.

## NUTRITIONAL ANALYSIS

**EACH WITH:** 230 g water; 201 calories (15% from fat, 47% from protein, 38% from carb); 24 g protein; 3 g total fat; 1 g saturated fat; 1 g monounsaturated fat; 1 g polyunsaturated fat; 19 g carb; 3 g fiber; 13 g sugar; 67 mg calcium; 2 mg iron; 65 mg sodium; 613 mg potassium; 2031 IU vitamin A; 91 mg vitamin C; 61 mg cholesterol

# Chicken and Dumplings

Yield: 6 servings

*Classic southern USA comfort food . . . good any time of year but especially as the weather gets cooler.*

- 1½ cups (165 g) chicken, cooked and cubed
- 3 cups (705 ml) low sodium chicken broth
- 3 cups (705 ml) water
- 1½ cups (195 g) carrot, sliced
- 4 medium potatoes, peeled and cubed
- 1 onion, chopped
- For dumplings:
- 2 cups (220 g) all-purpose flour
- 1 tablespoon (14 g) sodium-free baking powder
- 6 tablespoons (85 g) unsalted butter
- ⅔ cup (157 ml) skim milk

Place chicken, broth, water, and vegetables in a large pan. Bring to boiling. To make the dumplings, stir together the dry ingredients. Cut in butter until mixture resembles coarse crumbs. Stir in liquid until dough holds together in a ball. Drop dumplings on top by tablespoonfuls. Reduce heat and simmer uncovered for 10 minutes. Cover and simmer for 10 minutes more.

## NUTRITIONAL ANALYSIS

**EACH WITH:** 489 g water; 546 calories (25% from fat, 16% from protein, 59% from carb); 22 g protein; 16 g total fat; 8 g saturated fat; 4 g monounsaturated fat; 1 g polyunsaturated fat; 81 g carb; 6 g fiber; 4 g sugar; 200 mg calcium; 4 mg iron; 122 mg sodium; 1325 mg potassium; 4287 IU vitamin A; 18 mg vitamin C; 62 mg cholesterol

# Chicken Paella

Yield: 6 servings

*A Spanish-flavored chicken and rice dish. This uses turmeric rather than the more traditional, and more expensive, saffron.*

1¼ pounds (570 g) boneless chicken breast, cut into strips

1 tablespoon (15 ml) olive oil

1 onion, chopped

2 cloves garlic, minced

2¼ cups (535 ml) low sodium chicken broth

1 cup (185 g) long-grain rice, uncooked

1 teaspoon dried oregano, crushed

½ teaspoon paprika

¼ teaspoon black pepper

⅛ teaspoon ground turmeric

2 cups (475 ml) low sodium stewed tomatoes

1 medium red bell pepper, cut into strips

¾ cup (98 g) frozen peas

In a 10-inch (25-cm) skillet, cook chicken, half at a time, in hot oil until no longer pink. Remove chicken from skillet. Add onion and garlic; cook until tender but not brown. Remove skillet from heat. Add broth, uncooked rice, oregano, paprika, black pepper, and turmeric. Bring to boiling. Reduce heat. Simmer covered for about 15 minutes. Add undrained tomatoes, bell pepper, and frozen peas to skillet. Cover and simmer about 5 minutes more or until rice is tender. Stir in cooked chicken until heated through.

NUTRITIONAL ANALYSIS

**EACH WITH:** 294 g water; 291 calories (12% from fat, 38% from protein, 49% from carb); 28 g protein; 4 g total fat; 1 g saturated fat; 2 g monounsaturated fat; 1 g polyunsaturated fat; 36 g carb; 3 g fiber; 5 g sugar; 66 mg calcium; 3 mg iron; 122 mg sodium; 652 mg potassium; 1434 IU vitamin A; 64 mg vitamin C; 55 mg cholesterol

# Chicken Shepherd's Pie

Yield: 6 servings

*This is one of those "variation" sorts of things. When I made it with chicken, it seemed to be more popular than the traditional hamburger version, but perhaps that's just because it was something different.*

2 tablespoons (16 g) cornstarch

1 cup (235 ml) low sodium chicken broth

1½ cups (165 g) chicken, cooked and diced

12 ounces (340 g) frozen mixed vegetables

3 cups (675 g) mashed potatoes

Mix the cornstarch with the broth. Heat until thickened and bubbly. Stir in chicken. Place in bottom of a 9 x 9-inch (23 x 23-cm) baking dish. Cook vegetables until almost tender. Spread over chicken mixture. Cover with prepared mashed potatoes. Heat under broiler until potatoes start to brown.

NUTRITIONAL ANALYSIS

**EACH WITH:** 110 g water; 201 calories (12% from fat, 29% from protein, 59% from carb); 14 g protein; 3 g total fat; 1 g saturated fat; 1 g monounsaturated fat; 1 g polyunsaturated fat; 29 g carb; 4 g fiber; 3 g sugar; 29 mg calcium; 1 mg iron; 92 mg sodium; 475 mg potassium; 21 IU vitamin A; 22 mg vitamin C; 31 mg cholesterol

# Slow-Cooker Curried Chicken

Yield: 5 servings

*Curries make a nice slow-cooker meal because they fill the house with such a great aroma. This one calls for a number of spices that are typical of curry powder. If you have a favorite curry powder on the shelf, you could substitute that for the other spices.*

5 medium potatoes, diced

1 green bell pepper, coarsely chopped

1 medium onion, coarsely chopped

1 pound (455 g) boneless chicken breast, cubed

2 cups (475 ml) no-salt-added tomatoes

1 tablespoon (6 g) coriander

1½ tablespoons (10.5 g) paprika

1 tablespoon (5.5 g) ground ginger

¼ teaspoon cayenne pepper

½ teaspoon turmeric

¼ teaspoon ground cinnamon

⅛ teaspoon cloves

1 cup (235 ml) low sodium chicken broth

2 tablespoons (28 ml) cold water

4 tablespoons (32 g) cornstarch

Place vegetables in slow cooker. Place chicken on top. Mix together tomatoes, spices, and chicken broth. Pour over chicken. Cook on low for 8 to 10 hours or on high for 5 to 6 hours. Remove meat and vegetables. Turn heat to high. Stir cornstarch into water. Add to slow cooker. Cook until sauce is slightly thickened, 15 to 20 minutes.

## NUTRITIONAL ANALYSIS

**EACH WITH:** 433 g water; 346 calories (3% from fat, 12% from protein, 85% from carb); 11 g protein; 1 g total fat; 0 g saturated fat; 0 g monounsaturated fat; 0 g polyunsaturated fat; 76 g carb; 8 g fiber; 7 g sugar; 77 mg calcium; 3 mg iron; 55 mg sodium; 1432 mg potassium; 1363 IU vitamin A; 65 mg vitamin C; 9 mg cholesterol

# Pasta with Chicken and Vegetables

Yield: 6 servings

*This is a good way to use up a few fresh vegetables. It makes a simple one-dish meal that's perfect for a warm evening with just a little homemade bread.*

8 ounces (230 g) linguine or spaghetti

2 tablespoons (30 ml) vegetable oil

2 small zucchini, cut into strips

½ cup (35 g) mushrooms, sliced

1 clove garlic, minced

½ teaspoon dried basil

1 cup (235 ml) skim milk

2 cups (220 g) chicken, cooked and cubed

⅛ teaspoon black pepper

6 roma tomatoes, sliced

2 tablespoons (10 g) Parmesan cheese, grated

Cook linguine or spaghetti according to package directions. In a skillet, heat the oil. Add the zucchini, mushrooms, garlic, and basil. Cook and stir until zucchini is crisp-tender, 2 to 3 minutes. Drain pasta and return to pan. Stir in milk, chicken, pepper, and zucchini mixture and heat through. Add tomatoes and cheese. Toss and serve.

## NUTRITIONAL ANALYSIS

**EACH WITH:** 76 g water; 301 calories (31% from fat, 29% from protein, 40% from carb); 21 g protein; 10 g total fat; 2 g saturated fat; 3 g monounsaturated fat; 4 g polyunsaturated fat; 30 g carb; 1 g fiber; 0 g sugar; 103 mg calcium; 1 mg iron; 104 mg sodium; 302 mg potassium; 146 IU vitamin A; 1 mg vitamin C; 80 mg cholesterol

# Chicken Pot Pie

Yield: 8 servings

*A chicken-and-dumplings variation that is topped with mashed potatoes. Make sure you read the label when you buy instant mashed potato flakes. Some brands contain large amounts of sodium. The figures included here assume eight servings of mashed potatoes, prepared according to package directions with unsalted butter and skim milk.*

1 chicken

2 cups (475 ml) low sodium chicken broth

1 onion, coarsely chopped

2 cups (260 g) carrot, sliced

6 ounces (170 g) no-salt-added frozen peas

1 tablespoon (0.4 g) dried parsley

1 teaspoon dried thyme

⅔ cup (73 g) all-purpose flour

1 cup (235 ml) water

6 cups (1350 g) mashed potatoes

Place chicken and broth in a slow cooker or Dutch oven and cook until chicken is done. Remove chicken from broth, debone, and chop coarsely. Strain fat from broth and add enough water to make 5 cups (1175 ml). Return broth to ovenproof Dutch oven. Add onion, carrot, peas, and spices and cook until carrots are tender. Add flour to water in a jar with a tight-fitting lid. Shake until dissolved. Add to broth and cook until thickened. Stir in chicken. Prepare mashed potatoes and drop onto top of chicken mixture. Place under broiler until potatoes start to brown.

**NUTRITIONAL ANALYSIS**

**EACH WITH:** 111 g water; 231 calories (4% from fat, 19% from protein, 77% from carb); 11 g protein; 1 g total fat; 0 g saturated fat; 0 g monounsaturated fat; 0 g polyunsaturated fat; 45 g carb; 5 g fiber; 4 g sugar; 36 mg calcium; 2 mg iron; 96 mg sodium; 609 mg potassium; 4360 IU vitamin A; 36 mg vitamin C; 17 mg cholesterol

# Turkey and Zucchini Meatloaf

Yield: 8 servings

*The glacé gives this a nice sweet-tart taste. The turkey is milder in flavor than beef, as well as being lower in fat.*

1¼ pounds (570 g) ground turkey

1 cup zucchini, grated

½ cup (60 g) low sodium bread crumbs

1 egg

1 tablespoon (0.4 g) dried parsley

½ teaspoon black pepper

½ teaspoon garlic powder

1 teaspoon onion powder

¼ cup (80 g) peach preserves

2 teaspoons (10 g) Dijon mustard

Preheat oven to 350°F (180°C, gas mark 4). Combine first 8 ingredients in a large bowl and mix well. Shape mixture into a loaf on a baking sheet. Bake for 45 minutes. Stir the preserves and the mustard together. Spread on top of the loaf. Return to oven until internal temperature is 165°F, about 20 minutes.

**NUTRITIONAL ANALYSIS**

**EACH WITH:** 71 g water; 191 calories (23% from fat, 49% from protein, 28% from carb); 23 g protein; 5 g total fat; 1 g saturated fat; 1 g monounsaturated fat; 1 g polyunsaturated fat; 13 g carb; 1 g fiber; 6 g sugar; 42 mg calcium; 2 mg iron; 68 mg sodium; 293 mg potassium; 108 IU vitamin A; 4 mg vitamin C; 85 mg cholesterol

# Chicken Gyros

Yield: 4 servings

*This is an easy-to-make and low sodium version of the classic Greek sandwich. Many markets carry unsalted pita bread, or you can find it online at SaltWatcher.com.*

- 2 boneless chicken breasts, cut into ½-inch (1¼-cm) strips
- 2 tablespoons (30 g) low sodium ketchup
- 2 tablespoons (30 ml) olive oil
- 1½ teaspoons white wine vinegar
- 1 teaspoon dried oregano
- 1 teaspoon dry mustard
- 1½ teaspoons curry powder
- 4 pita breads, cut in half
- 1½ cups (30 g) lettuce, shredded
- ½ cup (90 g) tomato, chopped
- 1 cup (230 g) plain low-fat yogurt

Place the chicken strips side by side in a glass baking dish. Stir together the ketchup, olive oil, white wine vinegar, oregano, mustard, and curry powder. Pour over the chicken in the dish. Allow the chicken to marinate while you preheat the oven's broiler. Broil uncovered for 15 minutes with the meat about 6 inches (15 cm) from the heat. Cook just until the chicken is cooked through, but not browned. Place hot chicken into pita pockets and spoon some of the juices from the pan over it. Top with lettuce, tomato, and yogurt.

## NUTRITIONAL ANALYSIS

**EACH WITH:** 133 g water; 325 calories (27% from fat, 21% from protein, 52% from carb); 17 g protein; 10 g total fat; 2 g saturated fat; 6 g monounsaturated fat; 42 g carb; 2 g Fiber;184 mg calcium; 3 mg iron; 93 mg sodium; 415 mg potassium; 341 IU vitamin A; 6 mg vitamin C; 26 mg cholesterol

# Chicken Salad

Yield: 4 servings

*This makes great sandwiches, and the food processor makes it easy. A few seconds will give you a perfectly ground and mixed salad.*

- 1 cup (110 g) chicken, cooked
- ¼ cup (25 g) celery, chopped
- 2 tablespoons (28 g) low sodium mayonnaise
- 2 tablespoons (30 g) sour cream
- ½ teaspoon onion powder

Place chicken and celery in food processor and process until finely ground. Add remaining ingredients and process until well mixed.

## NUTRITIONAL ANALYSIS

**EACH WITH:** 36 g water; 133 calories (65% from fat, 32% from protein, 3% from carb); 11 g protein; 10 g total fat; 2 g saturated fat; 3 g monounsaturated fat; 3 g polyunsaturated fat; 1 g carb; 0 g fiber; 0 g sugar; 19 mg calcium; 0 mg iron; 42 mg sodium; 120 mg potassium; 118 IU vitamin A; 0 mg vitamin C; 38 mg cholesterol

## TIP

I often cook a whole chicken or large batch of chicken parts in the slow cooker and then use the meat for this and other recipes.

# CHAPTER 7

# Beef

---

*"Beef … It's what's for dinner." At least that's what the beef producers' ads tell you. And I have to admit that it is often true for us. We probably eat more red meat than is ideal. If you are like that, you probably want to make sure that you are careful with portion sizes. You'll notice that we often opt for the leaner cuts like round steak over chuck and other fattier cuts. The ground beef is 90 to 93 percent lean. If you buy less lean cuts than this, be aware that it will add to the fat and the calories in the recipes. This chapter contains a variety of beef recipes, from burgers to steaks, with a good assortment of oven-roasted and slow-cooker recipes mixed in.*

# Barbecued Steak

Yield: 4 servings

*Now I happen to be one of those people who usually feel a little pepper is the only thing a good steak needs. Steak sauce is one thing I never missed because I never used it. But I have to admit that a steak done up this way is maybe even better than a plain one. Give it a try and see if you agree.*

1½ pounds (680 g) beefsteak

1 clove garlic, cut in half

2 teaspoons (3.4 g) black peppercorns, crushed

¼ cup (55 g) unsalted butter

1 tablespoon (15 g) Dijon mustard

2 teaspoons (10 ml) Worcestershire sauce

½ teaspoon lime juice

Trim fat on beefsteak to ¼-inch (0.64-cm) thickness. Rub garlic on beef. Press peppercorns into beef. Mix together the butter, mustard, Worcestershire sauce, and lime juice. Heat coals or gas grill. Apply sauce to steak; cover, and grill beef 4 to 5 inches (10 to 13 cm) from medium heat. Turn steaks and apply sauce again; cook until desired doneness.

## NUTRITIONAL ANALYSIS

**EACH WITH:** 115 g water; 437 calories (52% from fat, 46% from protein, 2% from carb); 50 g protein; 25 g total fat; 12 g saturated fat; 8 g monounsaturated fat; 1 g polyunsaturated fat; 2 g carb; 0 g fiber; 0 g sugar; 40 mg calcium; 4 mg iron; 114 mg sodium; 652 mg potassium; 366 IU vitamin A; 5 mg vitamin C; 161 mg cholesterol

# Barbecued Beef Brisket

Yield: 10 servings

*I cooked this on the grill rather than in the oven. The flavor was great and it was falling-apart tender. The next day I had leftover beef on a leftover sesame seed bun for lunch.*

3 pounds (1¼ kg) beef brisket

FOR SAUCE:

1½ cups (240 g) onion, chopped

2 tablespoons (30 g) honey mustard

2 tablespoons (30 g) brown sugar

1 tablespoon (15 ml) Worcestershire sauce

1 teaspoon chili powder

¼ cup (60 ml) red wine

¼ cup (61 g) no-salt-added tomato sauce

2 tablespoons (40 g) molasses

Preheat the oven to 325°F (170°C, gas mark 3). Place a 24-inch (60-cm) length of heavy-duty aluminum foil in a 13 x 9-inch (33 x 23-cm) baking pan. Combine all the sauce ingredients in a medium bowl. Place the brisket in the center of the foil. Pour the sauce over the meat. Bring the ends of the foil together; fold the sides up to make a neatly sealed package. Bake for 3 to 3½ hours, or until the meat is tender. Remove from the oven. Trim any excess fat and thinly slice the meat across the grain. Skim the fat from the sauce with a spoon or fat separator. Serve the defatted gravy over the meat.

## NUTRITIONAL ANALYSIS

**EACH WITH:** 116 g water; 420 calories (67% from fat, 24% from protein, 9% from carb); 25 g protein; 30 g total fat; 12 g saturated fat; 13 g monounsaturated fat; 1 g polyunsaturated fat; 9 g carb; 1 g fiber; 6 g sugar; 43 mg calcium; 3 mg iron; 92 mg sodium; 532 mg potassium; 102 IU vitamin A; 5 mg vitamin C; 110 mg cholesterol

# Ribs with Barbecue Sauce

Yield: 4 servings

*I came across this sauce and had it in my "curiosity" file for months. When I finally tried it, I was sorry I'd waited so long. It's tomatoey, but neither sweet nor very spicy. The flavor is better the longer it sits, so it's worth the effort.*

- 3 ounces (90 ml) beer
- ½ teaspoon brown sugar
- 3 tablespoons (45 ml) vinegar
- 2 tablespoons (32 g) no-salt tomato paste
- ¼ cup (61 g) no-salt-added tomato sauce
- ¼ teaspoon dry mustard
- ½ teaspoon garlic powder
- ⅛ teaspoon dried sage
- ⅛ teaspoon dried oregano
- 1 tablespoon (7 g) Italian seasoning
- ⅛ teaspoon caraway seed
- ½ teaspoon dill weed
- ¼ teaspoon dried rosemary
- ¼ teaspoon cilantro
- ¼ teaspoon dried basil
- ⅛ teaspoon ground ginger
- 1 tablespoon (15 ml) Worcestershire sauce
- 1 teaspoon ground cinnamon
- 1 teaspoon hot pepper sauce
- 1 tablespoon (15 ml) liquid smoke
- 2 pounds (910 g) beef ribs

Combine all ingredients except ribs. Allow to sit overnight to develop flavor. Grill the ribs or cover with foil and cook in a 350°F (180°C, gas mark 4) oven until done, 1½ to 2 hours, basting with sauce occasionally.

**NUTRITIONAL ANALYSIS**

**EACH WITH:** 210 g water; 394 calories (45% from fat, 48% from protein, 7% from carb); 46 g protein; 19 g total fat; 8 g saturated fat; 8 g monounsaturated fat; 1 g polyunsaturated fat; 6 g carb; 1 g fiber; 3 g sugar; 50 mg calcium; 6 mg iron; 181 mg sodium; 1017 mg potassium; 275 IU vitamin A; 11 mg vitamin C; 134 mg cholesterol

# Gourmet Burgers

Yield: 4 servings

*Fresh ground beef works better than previously frozen for this recipe. Don't succumb to the bread-crumbs-and-eggs suggestions for burgers. That's just filler . . . we have a separate recipe for meat loaf.*

- 1¼ pounds (570 g) ground beef
- ¼ teaspoon garlic powder
- ½ teaspoon onion powder
- 1 tablespoon (15 ml) Worcestershire sauce
- 2 tablespoons (30 g) Dijon mustard
- ½ teaspoon black pepper, freshly ground

Mix all ingredients together. Form into 4 patties, taking care not to compress them more than necessary. Grill or panfry.

**NUTRITIONAL ANALYSIS**

**EACH WITH:** 89 g water; 372 calories (58% from fat, 40% from protein, 2% from carb); 36 g protein; 24 g total fat; 9 g saturated fat; 10 g monounsaturated fat; 1 g polyunsaturated fat; 2 g carb; 0 g fiber; 0 g sugar; 19 mg calcium; 4 mg iron; 117 mg sodium; 492 mg potassium; 15 IU vitamin A; 7 mg vitamin C; 115 mg cholesterol

# Asian Burgers

Yield: 6 servings

*There used to be a packaged mix for these, as well as a number of other Asian dishes, but they seem to have faded from the scene before I had a chance to banish them because of the sodium content. I don't know what it was, but it had to be bad. These are not.*

1½ pounds (680 g) ground beef

2 cups (500 g) oriental vegetable mix, drained

½ teaspoon Asian Seasoning mixture (see recipe, page 16)

¼ teaspoon ground ginger

¼ cup (60 ml) Soy Sauce Substitute (see recipe, page 28)

Combine all ingredients. Shape into 6 patties. Grill or fry to desired doneness.

### NUTRITIONAL ANALYSIS

**EACH WITH:** 100 g water; 326 calories (51% from fat, 41% from protein, 8% from carb); 32 g protein; 18 g total fat; 7 g saturated fat; 8 g monounsaturated fat; 1 g polyunsaturated fat; 6 g carb; 2 g fiber; 1 g sugar; 22 mg calcium; 3 mg iron; 87 mg sodium; 446 mg potassium; 0 IU vitamin A; 1 mg vitamin C; 98 mg cholesterol

# Cindy's Meat Loaf

Yield: 6 servings

*I got this recipe from a friend in Arkansas before I went on the low sodium diet, and it became an instant family favorite. Now I've eliminated the salt in the meat mixture and use no-salt-added tomato sauce. The sauce is the real star here, a sweet-and-sour bar-becuey marvel that gives the whole house a wonderful aroma while it cooks. I always make at least a double recipe, because it makes great sandwiches.*

1½ pounds (680 g) ground beef

1 cup (115 g) low sodium bread crumbs

1 onion, finely chopped

1 egg

¼ teaspoon black pepper

8 ounces (230 g) no-salt-added tomato sauce

½ cup (120 ml) water

2 teaspoons (10 ml) Worcestershire sauce

3 tablespoons (45 ml) vinegar

2 tablespoons (30 ml) mustard

3 tablespoons (45 g) brown sugar

Mix together beef, bread crumbs, onion, egg, and pepper and one-half the tomato sauce. Form into 1 large loaf or 2 small ones. Mix remaining ingredients together and pour over loaves. Bake at 350°F for 1½ hours.

### NUTRITIONAL ANALYSIS

**EACH WITH:** 157 g water; 429 calories (44% from fat, 31% from protein, 24% from carb); 33 g protein; 21 g total fat; 8 g saturated fat; 9 g monounsaturated fat; 1 g polyunsaturated fat; 26 g carb; 2 g fiber; 11 g sugar; 67 mg calcium; 4 mg iron; 116 mg sodium; 625 mg potassium; 188 IU vitamin A; 9 mg vitamin C; 133 mg cholesterol

# Sloppy Joes

Yield: 8 servings

*This is another quick sandwich meal that will cook while you are out. Small children and teenagers seem to like this too, so it's great for a party or family get-together.*

- 1½ pounds (680 g) ground beef
- 1 onion, chopped
- 1 cup (240 g) low sodium ketchup
- 1 green bell pepper, chopped
- 2 tablespoons (30 g) brown sugar
- ½ teaspoon garlic powder
- 2 tablespoons (30 g) prepared mustard
- 3 tablespoons (45 ml) vinegar
- 1 tablespoon (15 ml) Worcestershire sauce
- 1 teaspoon chili powder

In a skillet, brown beef and onion. Drain. Stir together remaining ingredients in slow cooker. Stir in meat and onion mixture. Cook on low for 6 to 8 hours or on high for 3 to 4 hours.

### NUTRITIONAL ANALYSIS

**EACH WITH:** 109 g water; 278 calories (46% from fat, 32% from protein, 22% from carb); 22 g protein; 14 g total fat; 6 g saturated fat; 6 g monounsaturated fat; 1 g polyunsaturated fat; 15 g carb; 1 g fiber; 12 g sugar; 24 mg calcium; 3 mg iron; 77 mg sodium; 511 mg potassium; 481 IU vitamin A; 24 mg vitamin C; 69 mg cholesterol

### TIP

Hunt's and Heinz both make a low sodium ketchup that seem to be pretty widely available in the United States.

# Meatballs

Yield: 6 servings

*These meatballs are good by themselves, but better if allowed to simmer in the sauce in a slow cooker for a few hours. Don't be afraid of the amount of onion in the sauce. The recipe has been modified to reduce the sodium with low sodium tomato paste, eliminating the salt and changing garlic salt to garlic powder.*

- 1½ pounds (680 g) ground beef
- 3 eggs
- ¼ cup (25 g) Parmesan cheese, grated
- ½ teaspoon garlic powder
- 1 tablespoon (4 g) dried parsley
- ½ tablespoon dried oregano
- 4 slices bread, low sodium, crumbled
- 3 onions, chopped
- 6 ounces (170 g) no-salt-added tomato paste
- 1½ cups (355 ml) water
- ½ cup (120 ml) red wine vinegar
- 3 tablespoons (45 g) brown sugar

Combine beef, eggs, cheese, seasonings, and bread. Form into 1-inch (2.5-cm) balls. Bake at 375°F (190°C, gas mark 5) for 30 to 40 minutes, turning once. Sauté onions in a few tablespoons of the meat drippings. Combine onions, tomato paste, water, vinegar, and brown sugar and place in slow cooker. Add meatballs. Stir to mix and cook on low for several hours.

### NUTRITIONAL ANALYSIS

**EACH WITH:** 242 g water; 429 calories (48% from fat, 33% from protein, 19% from carb); 35 g protein; 23 g total fat; 9 g saturated fat; 10 g monounsaturated fat; 1 g polyunsaturated fat; 20 g carb; 2 g fiber; 14 g sugar; 106 mg calcium; 5 mg iron; 218 mg sodium; 827 mg potassium; 663 IU vitamin A; 11 mg vitamin C; 219 mg cholesterol

# Salisbury Steak

Yield: 4 servings

*Another comfort food. Perfect with mashed potatoes.*

2 tablespoons (16 g) all-purpose flour

1½ cups (355 ml) low sodium beef broth

1½ pounds (680 g) ground beef

1 cup (70 g) mushrooms, chopped

Mix together the flour and broth until blended. Form the beef into 4 patties. Brown lightly on each side. Add the broth mixture and mushrooms and simmer until the gravy is thickened and the beef is done.

### NUTRITIONAL ANALYSIS

**EACH WITH:** 202 g water; 458 calories (57% from fat, 40% from protein, 3% from carb); 45 g protein; 28 g total fat; 11 g saturated fat; 12 g monounsaturated fat; 1 g polyunsaturated fat; 4 g carb; 0 g fiber; 0 g sugar; 20 mg calcium; 5 mg iron; 155 mg sodium; 666 mg potassium; 0 IU vitamin A; 1 mg vitamin C; 138 mg cholesterol

# Beef Pot Roast

Yield: 6 servings

*In this classic pot roast with vegetables, we've reduced the fat by using round steak rather than the more common chuck.*

2 pounds (910 g) beef round steak

2 cups (475 ml) low sodium beef broth

1 onion, quartered

1 cup (130 g) carrot, sliced

6 medium potatoes, peeled and cut into large pieces

8 ounces (225 g) mushrooms, cut in half

Place all ingredients in a roasting pan. Cover and cook in a 325°F (170°C, gas mark 3) oven until tender, about 2 hours.

### NUTRITIONAL ANALYSIS

**EACH WITH:** 372 g water; 466 calories (15% from fat, 53% from protein, 32% from carb); 61 g protein; 8 g total fat; 3 g saturated fat; 3 g monounsaturated fat; 0 g polyunsaturated fat; 36 g carb; 4 g fiber; 4 g sugar; 47 mg calcium; 7 mg iron; 125 mg sodium; 1498 mg potassium; 2570 IU vitamin A; 37 mg vitamin C; 136 mg cholesterol

# Beef and Cabbage Stew

Yield: 5 servings

*When you start looking, it's amazing how many recipes you find where you say, "Why haven't we made that again lately?" This was a great-tasting, easy-to-make recipe from way back at the beginning of my low sodium days.*

2 tablespoons (16 g) all-purpose flour

¼ teaspoon black pepper

1½ pounds (680 g) round steak

2 tablespoons (30 ml) vegetable oil

3 onions, sliced

2 potatoes, cut into ½-inch (1¼-cm) cubes

¾ cup (175 ml) water

1 tablespoon (15 ml) vinegar

2 teaspoons (10 ml) low sodium beef bouillon

1 small cabbage

Combine flour and pepper. Coat meat with mixture. In a skillet, brown meat in oil on all sides. Transfer to crockery cooker and add onions and potatoes. Add water, vinegar, and bouillon to skillet. Stir, scraping up browned bits from bottom. Pour over beef and onions in cooker. Cover and cook on low for 8 hours. Serve over hot cooked cabbage wedges.

## NUTRITIONAL ANALYSIS

**EACH WITH:** 470 g water; 522 calories (29% from fat, 38% from protein, 34% from carb); 49 g protein; 17 g total fat; 4 g saturated fat; 6 g monounsaturated fat; 4 g polyunsaturated fat; 44 g carb; 8 g fiber; 5 g sugar; 127 mg calcium; 7 mg iron; 125 mg sodium; 1654 mg potassium; 246 IU vitamin A; 126 mg vitamin C; 131 mg cholesterol

# Beef Goulash

Yield: 8 servings

*This is great comfort food, perfect for winter or those last cold rainy days of early spring.*

5 tablespoons (40 g) all-purpose flour, divided

¼ teaspoon black pepper

2 pounds (910 g) beef stew meat, cubed

2 tablespoons (30 ml) vegetable oil

2 onions, sliced

1 cup (235 ml) water

1 cup (235 ml) apple juice

2 rutabagas, cubed

2 cups (260 g) carrots, sliced

½ teaspoon marjoram

½ teaspoon dried thyme

⅓ cup (80 ml) water

6 small potatoes, cooked and mashed

In a plastic bag, combine 2 tablespoons (16 g) of the flour and the pepper. Add meat and shake to coat. Heat oil in a Dutch oven. Brown the meat on all sides. Add onions, water, and apple juice. Cover and simmer until meat is nearly tender, 1 to 1½ hours. Add rutabagas, carrots, and spices. Cover and simmer an additional 30 minutes or until meat and veggies are tender. Blend the remaining 3 tablespoons (24 g) flour into the water and add to the mixture. Cook until thickened and bubbly. Serve with mashed potatoes.

## NUTRITIONAL ANALYSIS

**EACH WITH:** 454 g water; 576 calories (36% from fat, 28% from protein, 36% from carb); 40 g protein; 23 g total fat; 8 g saturated fat; 9 g monounsaturated fat; 3 g polyunsaturated fat; 52 g carb; 8 g fiber; 18 g sugar; 141 mg calcium; 7 mg iron; 141 mg sodium; 1671 mg potassium; 3863 IU vitamin A; 77 mg vitamin C; 113 mg cholesterol

# Beef Burgundy

Yield: **8 servings**

*A great beef and noodles dish, so easy to prepare in your slow cooker. The beef gets very tender from the long cooking process.*

4 slices low sodium bacon

2 pounds (910 g) beef stew meat

1 cup (130 g) carrots, cut into chunks

1 onion, sliced

½ cup (60 g) all-purpose flour

½ teaspoon marjoram

¼ teaspoon garlic powder

¼ teaspoon black pepper

1 cup (235 ml) low sodium beef broth

½ cup (120 ml) burgundy wine

1 tablespoon (15 ml) Worcestershire sauce

3 cups (210 g) mushrooms, sliced

16 ounces (455 g) egg noodles, uncooked

2 tablespoons (8 g) fresh parsley, optional

Cook bacon until crisp; drain and crumble. Place beef, bacon, carrots, and onion in the bottom of the slow cooker. Whisk together the flour, marjoram, garlic powder, and pepper with the broth, wine, and Worcestershire sauce. Pour the mixture into the slow cooker. Cook on high for 1 hour. Reduce to low and cook for 5 to 6 hours. Add mushrooms to slow cooker. Cook on high for 30 minutes or until mushrooms are tender. While mushrooms are cooking, prepare noodles according to package directions. Serve beef over noodles garnished with parsley, if desired.

NUTRITIONAL ANALYSIS

**EACH WITH:** 195 g water; 476 calories (43% from fat, 35% from protein, 22% from carb); 40 g protein; 22 g total fat; 8 g saturated fat; 9 g monounsaturated fat; 1 g polyunsaturated fat; 25 g carb; 1 g fiber; 2 g sugar; 32 mg calcium; 5 mg iron; 140 mg sodium; 563 mg potassium; 2023 IU vitamin A; 7 mg vitamin C; 137 mg cholesterol

# Slow-Cooker Beef Barbecue

Yield: **8 servings**

*A quick and easy way to have shredded beef barbecue sandwiches for dinner. Put this in the slow cooker and some rolls in the bread machine and when you get home, dinner will be almost done.*

1 large onion

2 pounds (910 g) beef chuck

½ teaspoon liquid smoke

1 cup (250 g) Barbecue Sauce (see recipe, page 24)

Slice onion and place in bottom of slow cooker. Place beef on top. Drizzle liquid smoke over. Cook on low for 10 to 12 hours. Remove meat and onion; drain and shred. Add sauce and mix well.

NUTRITIONAL ANALYSIS

**EACH WITH:** 93 g water; 406 calories (62% from fat, 32% from protein, 6% from carb); 32 g protein; 28 g total fat; 11 g saturated fat; 12 g monounsaturated fat; 1 g polyunsaturated fat; 6 g carb; 1 g fiber; 3 g sugar; 21 mg calcium; 4 mg iron; 118 mg sodium; 355 mg potassium; 7 IU vitamin A; 3 mg vitamin C; 112 mg cholesterol

# East Texas Skillet Meal

Yield: 4 servings

*This was sent in by newsletter reader LeJean. It makes a nice meal-in-a-pot sort of dinner. I made a meatless variation of it for lunch that was every bit as good.*

1 pound (455 g) ground beef

1 onion, chopped

1 tablespoon (10 g) garlic, minced

2 cups (475 ml) no-salt-added tomatoes

2 cups (200 g) black-eyed peas, cooked and drained

1½ teaspoons Cajun Seasoning (see recipe, page 20)

½ cup (70 g) cornmeal

½ cup (60 g) all-purpose flour

3 teaspoons (14 g) sodium-free baking powder

1 egg

½ cup (120 ml) skim milk

In a large cast iron or ovenproof skillet, brown ground beef, onion, and garlic. Add undrained tomatoes, black-eyed peas, and seasoning. Stir well. Combine cornmeal, flour, and baking powder. Stir together the egg and milk. Add to cornmeal mixture and stir until just moistened. Top ground beef mixture with cornbread batter and cook in 425°F (220°C, gas mark 7) oven for 20 to 25 minutes, or until cornbread is golden brown.

**NUTRITIONAL ANALYSIS**

**EACH WITH:** 305 g water; 598 calories (32% from fat, 29% from protein, 39% from carb); 43 g protein; 21 g total fat; 8 g saturated fat; 9 g monounsaturated fat; 1 g polyunsaturated fat; 58 g carb; 9 g fiber; 9 g sugar; 291 mg calcium; 7 mg iron; 140 mg sodium; 1496 mg potassium; 392 IU vitamin A; 22 mg vitamin C; 154 mg cholesterol

# Hungarian Beef Stew

Yield: 6 servings

*The kind of slow-cooker meal that greets you with a wonderful aroma with you return home from work. Stick a loaf of bread in the bread machine on timed bake and you have an instant dinner.*

2 pounds (910 g) round steak, cubed

6 medium potatoes, cut into ¾-inch (2-cm) pieces

1 cup (160 g) frozen pearl onions

¼ cup (28 g) all-purpose flour

1 tablespoon (7 g) paprika

½ teaspoon black pepper

¼ teaspoon caraway seed

2 cups (475 ml) low sodium beef broth

1 cup (130 g) no-salt-added frozen peas

½ cup (115 g) sour cream

Toss the beef, potatoes, onions, flour, and spices in the slow cooker. Pour the beef broth over top. Cover and cook on low for 7 to 8 hours. Stir in the peas and sour cream. Cover and cook on low about 15 minutes longer, until peas are tender.

**NUTRITIONAL ANALYSIS**

**EACH WITH:** 523 g water; 674 calories (22% from fat, 35% from protein, 43% from carb); 59 g protein; 16 g total fat; 7 g saturated fat; 6 g monounsaturated fat; 1 g polyunsaturated fat; 71 g carb; 9 g fiber; 6 g sugar; 90 mg calcium; 9 mg iron; 162 mg sodium; 2344 mg potassium; 1318 IU vitamin A; 78 mg vitamin C; 154 mg cholesterol

# Layered Hamburger Casserole

Yield: 6 servings

*This was originally a last-minute throw-together meal that turned out well enough to include here. It's quick to put together, although it takes a while to bake, so you can go off and do something else.*

1½ pounds (680 g) ground beef

1 onion, chopped

4 medium potatoes, thinly sliced

12 ounces (340 g) frozen corn

1 cup (235 ml) low sodium beef broth

1 cup (110 g) Swiss cheese, shredded

Brown beef and onion in a skillet. Place in the bottom of a 9 x 13-inch (23 x 33-cm) baking dish. Layer potatoes and corn on top of beef. Pour broth over all. Sprinkle cheese over top. Bake at 375°F (190°C, gas mark 5) until potatoes are tender, about an hour.

## NUTRITIONAL ANALYSIS

**EACH WITH:** 320 g water; 521 calories (33% from fat, 26% from protein, 40% from carb); 34 g protein; 20 g total fat; 7 g saturated fat; 8 g monounsaturated fat; 1 g polyunsaturated fat; 53 g carb; 5 g fiber; 4 g sugar; 33 mg calcium; 4 mg iron; 114 mg sodium; 1225 mg potassium; 124 IU vitamin A; 20 mg vitamin C; 92 mg cholesterol

# Stuffed Zucchini

Yield: 6 servings

*This is perfect for those times when you don't get back to check the garden as often as you should and find a couple of zucchini that would make great softball bats. Discard the seeds and any center part of the squash that has gotten hard or stringy and put the rest of what you scoop out into the filling.*

3 large zucchini

1¼ pounds (570 g) ground beef

1 onion, chopped

1 clove garlic, crushed

2 cups (475 ml) no-salt-added tomatoes

1½ cups (75 g) cooked rice or small pasta

1 teaspoon dried basil

6 ounces (170 g) Swiss cheese, sliced

Cut the zucchini in half lengthwise. Scrape out the center, leaving a thickness of about a half inch (1¼ cm). Discard the seeds and chop the remainder. Cook the meat, onion, and garlic in a large skillet until meat is done. Stir in tomatoes, rice or pasta, basil, and chopped zucchini. Cook the zucchini shells in boiling water until they begin to soften. Drain and place in baking pan. Divide the filling between the zucchini. Place 2 slices of cheese on top of each. Place under broiler until cheese is melted and bubbly.

## NUTRITIONAL ANALYSIS

**EACH WITH:** 366 g water; 452 calories (47% from fat, 32% from protein, 21% from carb); 36 g protein; 24 g total fat; 11 g saturated fat; 9 g monounsaturated fat; 1 g polyunsaturated fat; 24 g carb; 3 g fiber; 7 g sugar; 347 mg calcium; 4 mg iron; 99 mg sodium; 1047 mg potassium; 720 IU vitamin A; 44 mg vitamin C; 103 mg cholesterol

# Shepherd's Pie with Cornbread Crust

Yield: 8 servings

*A meal in a pan. This one makes a lot, so it's good for when you have the family all together or if you want some leftovers for lunch. The cornbread on the bottom adds some substance to this while adding minimum fat and sodium.*

1 pound (455 g) ground beef

1 medium onion, chopped

12 ounces (340 g) frozen mixed vegetables

3 cups (675 g) mashed potatoes, prepared according to package directions

4 ounces (115 g) Swiss cheese, shredded

For cornbread crust:

1 cup (110 g) all-purpose flour

¾ cup (105 g) cornmeal

1 tablespoon (13 g) sugar

2 teaspoons (9 g) sodium-free baking powder

1 cup (235 ml) skim milk

1 egg

2 tablespoons (28 ml) vegetable oil

Sauté beef and onion. Drain. Cook vegetables until almost done. Drain. To make crust, stir together flour, cornmeal, sugar, and baking powder. Combine milk, egg, and oil. Stir into dry ingredients until just mixed. Spread cornbread in the bottom of a 9 x 13-inch (23 x 33-cm) baking dish sprayed with nonstick vegetable oil spray. On top of cornbread, layer meat mixture, veggies, and potatoes. Sprinkle with cheese. Bake at 425°F (220°C, gas mark 7) for 20 minutes.

## NUTRITIONAL ANALYSIS

**EACH WITH:** 119 g water; 391 calories (32% from fat, 22% from protein, 46% from carb); 21 g protein; 14 g total fat; 4 g saturated fat; 5 g monounsaturated fat; 3 g polyunsaturated fat; 44 g carb; 4 g fiber; 4 g sugar; 127 mg calcium; 3 mg iron; 104 mg sodium; 689 mg potassium; 118 IU vitamin A; 18 mg vitamin C; 77 mg cholesterol

## TIP

This could also be cooked during the day in the slow cooker. Place the vegetables on the bottom, top with the browned meat mixture. Pour the broth over and sprinkle with the cheese. Cook on low for 6 to 8 minute.

# CHAPTER 8

# Pork

*Pork has a traditional reputation as being unhealthy because of the fat it contains. However, as the ads about "the other white meat" have told us, today's pork is leaner and better for us than it used to be. You still need to be careful on several fronts here, though. First, not all cuts of pork are lean, so be choosy when you buy. Second, like poultry, pork is more and more often being "enhanced" with a solution that contains salt. In the case of one store, I've even seen pork that was labeled enhanced and did not contain a nutritional label, so it was impossible to know how much sodium was in it. As with everything, the best advice is to read the labels carefully.*

# Barbecued Spareribs

Yield: 4 servings

*These ribs are done in the traditional way, cooked most of the way with just a spice rub and then "mopped" with sauce near the end. This helps to keep the meat from getting too dried out. I personally prefer to smoke the ribs until they are nearly done, then move them to the grill for the last 20 minutes or so to sear the sauce into them.*

2 pounds (910 g) pork spareribs

¼ cup (60 ml) cider vinegar

FOR RUB:

½ cup (115 g) brown sugar

1½ teaspoons black pepper

1 teaspoon cayenne pepper

FOR SAUCE:

8 ounces (230 g) no-salt-added tomato sauce

½ cup (120 ml) cider vinegar

¼ cup (85 g) honey

1 teaspoon onion powder

1 teaspoon dry mustard

1 teaspoon garlic powder

½ teaspoon cayenne pepper

Brush ribs with vinegar. Mix rub ingredients together and rub into ribs. Smoke or grill until done. While ribs are cooking, combine sauce ingredients. Brush with sauce during the last half hour of cooking.

**NUTRITIONAL ANALYSIS**

**EACH WITH:** 162 g water; 529 calories (45% from fat, 15% from protein, 39% from carb); 21 g protein; 27 g total fat; 10 g saturated fat; 12 g monounsaturated fat; 3 g polyunsaturated fat; 53 g carb; 1 g fiber; 49 g sugar; 78 mg calcium; 3 mg iron; 106 mg sodium; 694 mg potassium; 487 IU vitamin A; 8 mg vitamin C; 88 mg cholesterol

# Honey-Glazed Spareribs

Yield: 4 servings

*These need to be slow cooked. I wouldn't turn the oven up higher than about 275 °F (140 °C, gas mark 1) if I did them that way. Too high a temperature and the honey will end up black and crispy. (Of course, some people like ribs that way.) I did these in the smoker and they turned out tender and juicy inside and just a little crisp outside. If you are not doing them in a smoker or over an indirect fire, you might also want to add a little liquid smoke to the glaze.*

2 pounds (910 g) pork spareribs

¼ cup (85 g) honey

2 tablespoons (14 g) paprika

¼ teaspoon cayenne pepper

½ teaspoon black pepper

½ teaspoon onion powder

¼ teaspoon garlic powder

Combine honey and spices. Brush on ribs. Smoke or cook slowly until done.

**NUTRITIONAL ANALYSIS**

**EACH WITH:** 69 g water; 401 calories (60% from fat, 20% from protein, 20% from carb); 20 g protein; 27 g total fat; 10 g saturated fat; 12 g monounsaturated fat; 3 g polyunsaturated fat; 20 g carb; 1 g fiber; 18 g sugar; 45 mg calcium; 2 mg iron; 89 mg sodium; 396 mg potassium; 1877 IU vitamin A; 3 mg vitamin C; 88 mg cholesterol

# Ranch Ribs

Yield: 6 servings

*"Ranch" in a way you may not have expected. When my son and daughter took over cooking one Sunday evening, they were looking for something a little different as a sauce for country-style ribs. The answer? Ranch dressing. And it was better than you can imagine.*

- **2 pounds (910 g) country-style ribs**
- **½ cup (115 g) peppercorn ranch dressing**

Grill ribs over medium coals until done, about an hour. Baste with dressing the last 15 minutes.

**NUTRITIONAL ANALYSIS**

**EACH WITH:** 108 g water; 416 calories (72% from fat, 25% from protein, 2% from carb); 26 g protein; 33 g total fat; 10 g saturated fat; 13 g monounsaturated fat; 3 g polyunsaturated fat; 2 g carb; 0 g fiber; 1 g sugar; 46 mg calcium; 1 mg iron; 108 mg sodium; 483 mg potassium; 20 IU vitamin A; 1 mg vitamin C; 110 mg cholesterol

# Apple Butter Ribs

Yield: 6 servings

*I found this recipe in a Betty Crocker cookbook and reworked it to reduce the sodium, lowering it from the 570 mg they had listed to 94 mg. Why would you want something sweet to be salty anyway?*

- **2 pounds (910 g) country-style ribs**
- **½ teaspoon black pepper**
- **1 onion, sliced**
- **½ cup (125 g) apple butter**
- **2 tablespoons (30 g) brown sugar**
- **1 tablespoon (15 ml) liquid smoke**
- **2 cloves garlic, minced**

Place ribs in slow cooker. Sprinkle with pepper. Cover with onion slices. Mix remaining ingredients and pour over. Cover and cook on low for 8 to 10 hours.

**NUTRITIONAL ANALYSIS**

**EACH WITH:** 128 g water; 433 calories (60% from fat, 24% from protein, 16% from carb); 26 g protein; 28 g total fat; 10 g saturated fat; 13 g monounsaturated fat; 3 g polyunsaturated fat; 17 g carb; 1 g fiber; 14 g sugar; 55 mg calcium; 2 mg iron; 94 mg sodium; 529 mg potassium; 15 IU vitamin A; 3 mg vitamin C; 104 mg cholesterol

# Pork for Subs

Yield: 4 servings

*Somehow I'd never really thought about roast pork as a sub filling. Here at the northern edge of the southern United States we have a lot barbecue carryouts and sliced, smoked pork is a favorite. That is the way I've usually made it, smoking a pork roast and slicing it for sandwiches with barbecue sauce. But on a trip to New York City I discovered Italian roast pork subs. This version cooks in the slow cooker while you are out. Slice it thinly and pile it on a homemade sub roll with a slice of low sodium Swiss cheese and a few sautéed onions and you have dinner.*

1 pound (455 g) pork loin

1½ teaspoons Italian seasoning

¼ teaspoon garlic powder

1 cup (235 ml) low sodium chicken broth

Place meat in slow cooker. Stir seasonings into broth and pour over. Cook on low for 8 to 10 hours or on high for 4 to 5 hours.

## NUTRITIONAL ANALYSIS

**EACH WITH:** 133 g water; 245 calories (60% from fat, 39% from protein, 1% from carb); 23 g protein; 16 g total fat; 6 g saturated fat; 7 g monounsaturated fat; 2 g polyunsaturated fat; 1 g carb; 0 g fiber; 0 g sugar; 17 mg calcium; 1 mg iron; 71 mg sodium; 495 mg potassium; 33 IU vitamin A; 1 mg vitamin C; 68 mg cholesterol

## TIP

Prices here for whole pork loins are often much lower than buying what you would think would be cheaper cuts of pork like regular pork chops, so you can buy one and slice it into chops and small roasts for just this kind of meal.

# Breaded Pork Chops

Yield: 4 servings

*You can easily vary the flavor of these chops by changing the seasonings. I was looking for a sort of Southern flavor, but you could just as easily make them Italian, Mexican, barbecue, or whatever you want.*

4 pork chops

½ cup (60 g) low sodium bread crumbs

1 tablespoon (0.4 g) dried parsley

½ teaspoon dried sage

½ teaspoon dried thyme

1 teaspoon white pepper

1 teaspoon onion powder

1 teaspoon dried basil

¼ teaspoon cayenne pepper

Nonstick vegetable oil spray

Moisten chops with water. Combine bread crumbs and spices in a resealable plastic bag. Add chops and shake until evenly covered. Spray a baking sheet with nonstick vegetable oil spray. Place the chops on the sheet and spray the tops with more of the vegetable oil spray. Bake at 350°F (180°C, gas mark 4) until done, 20 to 30 minutes depending on thickness of chops.

## NUTRITIONAL ANALYSIS

**EACH WITH:** 43 g water; 315 calories (60% from fat, 26% from protein, 14% from carb); 20 g protein; 21 g total fat; 8 g saturated fat; 9 g monounsaturated fat; 2 g polyunsaturated fat; 11 g carb; 1 g fiber; 1 g sugar; 60 mg calcium; 2 mg iron; 62 mg sodium; 323 mg potassium; 157 IU vitamin A; 2 mg vitamin C; 69 mg cholesterol

# Ginger-Apple Braised Pork Chops

Yield: 3 servings

*This recipe comes from subscriber Margaret. We tried it and it is truly delicious. It's just spicy enough to satisfy even those people who aren't on a low sodium diet.*

½ cup (80 g) onion, chopped

2 tablespoons (30 ml) olive oil

3 pork chops

2 tablespoons (12.5 g) fresh ginger, thinly sliced

1 apple, peeled and thinly sliced

½ cup (120 ml) water

Lightly brown the chopped onion in the olive oil; using medium heat in a nonstick skillet, 2 to 4 minutes. Push the onion pieces to one side and brown the chops on each side. Spoon the onion pieces on top of each chop, dividing evenly. Peel and slice the ginger and apple while the chops are browning. Then layer each chop with a topping of sliced ginger and apple. Add the water to the skillet and cover tightly. Cook over low heat for 30 to 40 minutes, depending on the thickness of the pork chops. Serve with the ginger-apple topping.

### NUTRITIONAL ANALYSIS

**EACH WITH:** 145 g water; 370 calories (71% from fat, 20% from protein, 10% from carb); 18 g protein; 29 g total fat; 9 g saturated fat; 15 g monounsaturated fat; 3 g polyunsaturated fat; 9 g carb; 1 g fiber; 6 g sugar; 33 mg calcium; 1 mg iron; 58 mg sodium; 369 mg potassium; 23 IU vitamin A; 4 mg vitamin C; 69 mg cholesterol

# Honey-Grilled Pork Chops

Yield: 4 servings

*A quick and easy grill recipe.*

2 tablespoons (40 g) honey

¼ cup (60 ml) Worcestershire sauce

¼ teaspoon black pepper

¼ teaspoon garlic powder

4 boneless pork chops

In a shallow glass dish or bowl, mix together honey, Worcestershire sauce, and spices. Add pork chops and toss to coat. Cover and refrigerate for no more than 4 hours to marinate. Lightly oil grill and preheat to medium. Remove pork chops from marinade. Grill until cooked through, 20 to 30 minutes, turning often.

### NUTRITIONAL ANALYSIS

**EACH WITH:** 69 g water; 179 calories (29% from fat, 44% from protein, 26% from carb); 20 g protein; 6 g total fat; 2 g saturated fat; 3 g monounsaturated fat; 1 g polyunsaturated fat; 12 g carb; 0 g fiber; 9 g sugar; 6 mg calcium; 2 mg iron; 100 mg sodium; 500 mg potassium; 23 IU vitamin A; 27 mg vitamin C; 48 mg cholesterol

### TIP

You could make a little extra of the marinade and put it on zucchini slices while they grill as a side dish.

# Pork Chop and Stuffing Bake

Yield: 4 servings

*A quick and easy sort of meal for those nights when you don't want to stand around in the kitchen for an hour. Toss it together, stick it in the oven, and return when it's ready to eat.*

4 pork chops

1 tablespoon (15 ml) vegetable oil

1 onion, chopped

½ cup (50 g) celery, chopped

1 apple, peeled, cored, and chopped

2 cups (475 ml) low sodium chicken broth

¼ cup (60 ml) skim milk

4 cups cubed low sodium bread

In a large skillet, brown pork chops on both sides in oil. Remove chops. Add onion and celery and cook until tender. Add apple and cook another minute. Stir in broth and milk. Heat to almost boiling. Stir in bread cubes. Place mixture in 13 x 9-inch (33 x 23-cm) baking dish. Place chops on top. Cover with foil and bake at 375°F (190°C, gas mark 5) for 30 to 40 minutes or until chops are cooked through.

**NUTRITIONAL ANALYSIS**

**EACH WITH:** 258 g water; 451 calories (50% from fat, 22% from protein, 28% from carb); 24 g protein; 25 g total fat; 8 g saturated fat; 10 g monounsaturated fat; 4 g polyunsaturated fat; 31 g carb; 2 g fiber; 7 g sugar; 118 mg calcium; 3 mg iron; 138 mg sodium; 570 mg potassium; 118 IU vitamin A; 5 mg vitamin C; 70 mg cholesterol

# Pork Stroganoff

Yield: 6 servings

*Even though beef is more traditional for stroganoff, this works well too. At least around here, you can buy a boneless pork loin for less than ground beef, or any other beef cut for that matter.*

1½ pounds (680 g) pork loin, cut in ¾-inch (2-cm) cubes

1 tablespoon (15 ml) vegetable oil

½ cup (80 g) onion, chopped

¼ teaspoon garlic powder

1 cup (235 ml) water

8 ounces (225 g) mushrooms, sliced

1 tablespoon (15 ml) low sodium beef bouillon

1 teaspoon dill weed

⅛ teaspoon black pepper

½ cup (115 g) sour cream

¼ cup (60 ml) white wine

3 tablespoons (24 g) all-purpose flour

In a skillet, brown the meat in the oil. Add the onion and cook until softened. Transfer to slow-cooker. Combine garlic powder, water, mushrooms, bouillon, and spices. Pour over meat mixture. Cook on low for 8 to 10 hours or on high for 5 to 6 hours. Turn heat to high. Stir together sour cream, wine, and flour. Add to slow cooker. Cook until sauce is thickened, 15 to 20 minutes.

**NUTRITIONAL ANALYSIS**

**EACH WITH:** 184 g water; 338 calories (61% from fat, 30% from protein, 9% from carb); 25 g protein; 22 g total fat; 8 g saturated fat; 9 g monounsaturated fat; 3 g polyunsaturated fat; 7 g carb; 1 g fiber; 1 g sugar; 38 mg calcium; 1 mg iron; 103 mg sodium; 632 mg potassium; 168 IU vitamin A; 3 mg vitamin C; 76 mg cholesterol

# Peasant Stew

Yield: 6 servings

*This was one of those difficult-to-name recipes. Somehow, I just seemed to picture a group of peasants in a Mary Shelley novel sitting down to steaming bowls after storming the castle by torchlight. It turned out surprisingly well, though . . . everyone was impressed with something I had just thrown in the slow cooker before going off to work.*

1½ pounds (680 g) pork loin

4 turnips, chopped

1½ cups (195 g) carrot, sliced

½ head cabbage, coarsely chopped

2 cups (475 ml) low sodium beef broth

2 cups (475 ml) no-salt-added tomatoes

1 tablespoon (10 g) minced onion

½ teaspoon garlic powder

1 tablespoon (0.4 g) dried parsley

½ teaspoon dried thyme

¼ cup (60 ml) white wine

Place pork in bottom of slow cooker. Cover with carrot and cabbage. Stir together remaining ingredients and pour over. Cook on low for 8 to 10 hours or on high for 4 to 5 hours. Remove pork, shred coarsely, and stir back into stew.

**NUTRITIONAL ANALYSIS**

**EACH WITH:** 389 g water; 150 calories (24% from fat, 24% from protein, 52% from carb); 9 g protein; 4 g total fat; 1 g saturated fat; 2 g monounsaturated fat; 1 g polyunsaturated fat; 20 g carb; 6 g fiber; 9 g sugar; 120 mg calcium; 2 mg iron; 169 mg sodium; 896 mg potassium; 4109 IU vitamin A; 79 mg vitamin C; 15 mg cholesterol

# Slow-Cooker Pork Stew

Yield: 4 servings

*It's nice to have dinner finished when you get home once in a while. You can serve this over rice or noodles or just have it with a big slice of freshly baked bread (the delay bake option goes so well with the slow cooker).*

1 pound (455 g) pork loin, cubed

1 onion

2 cups (475 ml) no-salt-added tomatoes

1 green bell pepper, coarsely chopped

2 cups (475 ml) low sodium chicken broth

8 ounces (225 g) mushrooms, quartered

1 tablespoon (0.4 g) dried parsley

1 teaspoon dried thyme

¼ cup (15 g) fresh cilantro

¼ cup (28 g) all-purpose flour

Cube pork. Layer all ingredients except flour in the slow cooker, reserving half the chicken broth. Cook on low for 6 to 8 hours. Stir the flour into the remaining chicken broth. Add to the cooker. Turn to high and cook an additional half hour or until slightly thickened.

**NUTRITIONAL ANALYSIS**

**EACH WITH:** 365 g water; 147 calories (24% from fat, 28% from protein, 48% from carb); 11 g protein; 4 g total fat; 1 g saturated fat; 2 g monounsaturated fat; 1 g polyunsaturated fat; 19 g carb; 3 g fiber; 7 g sugar; 68 mg calcium; 2 mg iron; 77 mg sodium; 789 mg potassium; 562 IU vitamin A; 53 mg vitamin C; 15 mg cholesterol

# Slow-Cooker Pork and Sweet Potatoes

Yield: 8 servings

*One of those meals that just takes too long to fix when you get home from work, transformed into an easy slow-cooker creation.*

4 sweet potatoes, peeled and sliced

2 pounds (910 g) pork loin roast

½ cup (115 g) brown sugar

¼ teaspoon cayenne pepper

¼ teaspoon black pepper

¼ teaspoon garlic powder

½ teaspoon onion powder

Place potatoes in bottom of a slow cooker. Place pork on top. Combine remaining ingredients and sprinkle over pork and potatoes. Cover and cook on low for 8 to 10 hours. Remove pork and slice. Serve juices over pork and potatoes.

### NUTRITIONAL ANALYSIS

**EACH WITH:** 144 g water; 256 calories (18% from fat, 40% from protein, 43% from carb); 25 g protein; 5 g total fat; 2 g saturated fat; 2 g monounsaturated fat; 1 g polyunsaturated fat; 27 g carb; 2 g fiber; 18 g sugar; 48 mg calcium; 2 mg iron; 84 mg sodium; 645 mg potassium; 31 IU vitamin A; 11 mg vitamin C; 71 mg cholesterol

# Pork Chili Verde

Yield: 6 servings

*A chili variation. This one does not contain tomatoes and has pork instead of the more traditional beef. If you can't find cannellini beans, which are an Italian white kidney bean, you can substitute any other white bean such as navy or great northern beans.*

3 cups (300 g) cannellini beans, cooked according to package directions

1 onion, chopped

2 cloves garlic, minced

4 ounces (115 g) chopped chiles

2 teaspoons (2 g) dried oregano

1½ teaspoons cumin

¼ teaspoon ground cloves

¼ teaspoon cayenne pepper

3 cups (450 g) cooked pork roast, diced

2 cups (475 ml) low sodium chicken broth

Combine all ingredients in a large pot and simmer gently for about 1 hour.

### NUTRITIONAL ANALYSIS

**EACH WITH:** 94 g water; 478 calories (15% from fat, 36% from protein, 50% from carb); 43 g protein; 8 g total fat; 3 g saturated fat; 3 g monounsaturated fat; 1 g polyunsaturated fat; 60 g carb; 24 g fiber; 4 g sugar; 171 mg calcium; 9 mg iron; 75 mg sodium; 1681 mg potassium; 289 IU vitamin A; 53 mg vitamin C; 60 mg cholesterol

# Pulled Pork

Yield: 8 servings

*An easy way to make pork barbecue, even if not quite the traditional slow-smoked kind.*

½ cup (120 ml) cider vinegar

¼ cup (40 g) chopped onion

1 teaspoon Worcestershire sauce

1 teaspoon hot pepper sauce

3 pounds (1¼ kg) pork shoulder roast boneless, trimmed, tied

½ tablespoon liquid smoke

1 tablespoon (13 g) sugar

1 teaspoon paprika

¼ teaspoon black pepper

2 tablespoons (30 g) low sodium ketchup

In a large bowl, combine cider vinegar, chopped onion, Worcestershire sauce, and hot pepper sauce. Add the pork roast, cover, and marinate in refrigerator for 6 to 10 hours. Turn occasionally to keep roast coated with marinade. Remove the pork from the marinade, scraping the onion back into the marinade. Lightly pat the roast dry with paper towels. Pour the marinade into a slow cooker and add the liquid smoke. Place a slow-cooker meat rack or ring of foil in the slow cooker. Combine the sugar, paprika, and pepper in a cup. Rub the pork roast with the sugar and spice mixture and place on the rack in slow cooker. Cover and cook on low for 7 to 9 hours, or until very tender. Transfer the pork to a cutting board; cover with foil to keep warm. Skim the fat from the surface of the cooking liquid. Stir in the ketchup; pour into a bowl. Using 2 forks, pull the pork apart into shreds, or chop the pork into small pieces. Serve the pork on buns. Serve the sauce separately.

### NUTRITIONAL ANALYSIS

**EACH WITH:** 145 g water; 268 calories (42% from fat, 51% from protein, 7% from carb); 33 g protein; 12 g total fat; 4 g saturated fat; 6 g monounsaturated fat; 1 g polyunsaturated fat; 4 g carb; 0 g fiber; 4 g sugar; 27 mg calcium; 2 mg iron; 137 mg sodium; 634 mg potassium; 211 IU vitamin A; 4 mg vitamin C; 114 mg cholesterol

# CHAPTER 9

# Fish and Seafood

---

*My family and I probably should eat fish more than we do. It seems to be one of those things that I don't think about when I'm planning dinner, but always enjoy when we do have it. Most of the recipes here are for cat fish, salmon, and tuna, which are the varieties of fish that we have most often. However, many of the recipes could just as easily use other fish if your favorites are different. Be careful with seafood—it has a lot of natural sodium and cholesterol. Rinsing in cold water will help to reduce the sodium below the listed level.*

# Tuna Steaks

Yield: 2 servings

*If you get them on sale, tuna steaks are one of the cheaper fish products you can buy. The key to cooking them is not to overcook them and dry them out. It's all right for them to be medium or even medium rare. Soaking them in a simple marinade as this recipe does also helps to keep them moist and flavorful.*

2 tablespoons (30 ml) olive oil

2 tablespoons (30 ml) lemon juice

6 ounces (170 g) tuna steaks

½ teaspoon black pepper, freshly ground

Combine the olive oil and lemon juice. Marinate the steaks in the mixture at least a half hour, turning occasionally. Heat a skillet over high heat. Add the steaks and cook for 2 minutes. Sprinkle with pepper, turn over, and cook for 2 minutes longer.

**NUTRITIONAL ANALYSIS**

**EACH WITH:** 72 g water; 247 calories (65% from fat, 33% from protein, 3% from carb); 20 g protein; 18 g total fat; 3 g saturated fat; 11 g monounsaturated fat; 3 g polyunsaturated fat; 2 g carb; 0 g fiber; 0 g sugar; 10 mg calcium; 1 mg iron; 34 mg sodium; 240 mg potassium; 1861 IU vitamin A; 7 mg vitamin C; 32 mg cholesterol

# Balsamic Grilled Tuna Steaks

Yield: 4 servings

*Tuna steaks get tough if you cook them too long, so take them off the grill while they are still pink in the center to keep them juicy.*

½ cup (120 ml) balsamic vinegar

2 tablespoons (26 g) sugar

1 tablespoon (7 g) Italian seasoning

½ teaspoon garlic powder

1 tablespoon (15 ml) olive oil

1 tablespoon lemon peel

1 pound (455 g) tuna steaks

1 tablespoon (15 ml) lemon juice

Combine all ingredients except tuna and lemon juice and pour in a glass baking dish. Add tuna and marinate 15 minutes, turned frequently. Heat grill to high. Place fish on grill and grill until medium doneness, about 3 minutes per side. Place on serving plates and squeeze lemon juice over.

**NUTRITIONAL ANALYSIS**

**EACH WITH:** 110 g water; 227 calories (36% from fat, 47% from protein, 17% from carb); 27 g protein; 9 g total fat; 2 g saturated fat; 4 g monounsaturated fat; 2 g polyunsaturated fat; 9 g carb; 1 g fiber; 8 g sugar; 25 mg calcium; 2 mg iron; 45 mg sodium; 339 mg potassium; 2529 IU vitamin A; 4 mg vitamin C; 43 mg cholesterol

# Beer-Battered Catfish

Yield: 4 servings

*Not particularly low in fat, but the batter has a nice flavor and sticks to the fish better than any other I've tried.*

½ cup (60 g) all-purpose flour

½ cup (70 g) cornmeal

1 teaspoon New Bay Seasoning (see recipe, page 17)

1 cup beer

1½ pounds (680 g) catfish fillets, cut into serving-size pieces

Vegetable oil for frying

Stir together flour, cornmeal, and seasoning. Add beer and stir until completely moistened. Dip fish pieces in batter. Deep-fry at 350°F (180°C, gas mark 4) until fish is done, about 5 minutes.

## NUTRITIONAL ANALYSIS

**EACH WITH:** 132 g water; 350 calories (35% from fat, 35% from protein, 30% from carb); 30 g protein; 13 g total fat; 3 g saturated fat; 6 g monounsaturated fat; 3 g polyunsaturated fat; 25 g carb; 2 g fiber; 0 g sugar; 19 mg calcium; 2 mg iron; 91 mg sodium; 553 mg potassium; 122 IU vitamin A; 1 mg vitamin C; 80 mg cholesterol

# Fried Catfish

Yield: 6 servings

*These can also be "fried" in the oven to reduce the fat content. Spray with nonstick vegetable oil spray and bake until browned and crispy.*

¼ cup (60 ml) evaporated milk

¼ teaspoon black pepper

½ cup (60 g) all-purpose flour

¼ cup (35 g) cornmeal

1 teaspoon paprika

1½ pounds (680 g) catfish fillets

Vegetable oil for frying

Combine milk and pepper. In a separate bowl, combine flour, cornmeal, and paprika. Dip fish in milk mixture and roll in flour mixture. Place about ½ inch (1¼ cm) of oil in a heavy skillet. Fry fish in hot fat for 4 minutes. Turn carefully and fry for 4 to 6 minutes longer or until fish is brown and flakes easily when tested with a fork.

## NUTRITIONAL ANALYSIS

**EACH WITH:** 98 g water; 324 calories (29% from fat, 28% from protein, 43% from carb); 22 g protein; 10 g total fat; 3 g saturated fat; 4 g monounsaturated fat; 2 g polyunsaturated fat; 34 g carb; 3 g fiber; 0 g sugar; 42 mg calcium; 3 mg iron; 73 mg sodium; 444 mg potassium; 370 IU vitamin A; 1 mg vitamin C; 56 mg cholesterol

# Potato-Crusted Fish

Yield: 4 servings

*A nice crunchy coating without fat or sodium. Goes really well with oven-fried potatoes.*

1 egg

2 tablespoons (28 ml) skim milk

½ cup (25 g) mashed potato flakes

¼ teaspoon black pepper

1 pound (455 g) catfish fillets

Nonstick vegetable oil spray

Mix egg and milk together. Stir together potato flakes and pepper. Dip fish in egg mixture, then potato flakes. Repeat. Place on baking sheet. Spray with nonstick vegetable oil spray until moistened. Bake at 325°F (170°C, gas mark 3) until fish flakes easily, about 15 minutes.

### NUTRITIONAL ANALYSIS

**EACH WITH:** 106 g water; 191 calories (44% from fat, 44% from protein, 12% from carb); 20 g protein; 9 g total fat; 2 g saturated fat; 4 g monounsaturated fat; 2 g polyunsaturated fat; 5 g carb; 0 g fiber; 0 g sugar; 32 mg calcium; 1 mg iron; 99 mg sodium; 472 mg potassium; 130 IU vitamin A; 6 mg vitamin C; 54 mg cholesterol

### TIP

Make sure the instant potato flakes you buy do not include added salt, as many of the "complete" mixes do.

# Balsamic and Maple Salmon

Yield: 2 servings

*One item that I find particularly useful is balsamic vinegar. It has more flavor and is less sour than other vinegars. And it has zero sodium, which makes it a great choice for sauces and marinades. In this recipe the tartness of the balsamic vinegar is paired with maple syrup. This gives the salmon a nice change of pace flavor-wise. The maple syrup goes well with the natural sweetness of the fish and the sauce doesn't add any sodium to the recipe.*

¼ cup (60 ml) balsamic vinegar

¼ cup (60 ml) water

2 tablespoons (28 ml) olive oil

2 tablespoons (28 ml) maple syrup

¼ teaspoon garlic powder

8 ounces (225 g) salmon fillets

Heat all ingredients except salmon in a large skillet, stirring to combine. Add salmon fillets. Cover and cook until salmon is done, about 10 minutes, turning once.

### NUTRITIONAL ANALYSIS

**EACH WITH:** 142 g water; 385 calories (60% from fat, 23% from protein, 16% from carb); 23 g protein; 26 g total fat; 4 g saturated fat; 14 g monounsaturated fat; 6 g polyunsaturated fat; 16 g carb; 0 g fiber; 14 g sugar; 30 mg calcium; 1 mg iron; 70 mg sodium; 486 mg potassium; 57 IU vitamin A; 4 mg vitamin C; 67 mg cholesterol

# Barbecued Salmon

Yield: 6 servings

*Use a whole salmon fillet for this recipe. It makes an impressive display and also stays juicier than smaller pieces would be. A low sodium barbecue sauce that would be more common for pork or chicken gives the salmon just enough of a sweet crustiness to hold those juices in.*

¼ cup (60 g) brown sugar

2 tablespoons (30 ml) cider vinegar

2 tablespoons (40 g) honey

¼ teaspoon liquid smoke

¼ teaspoon black pepper

1 clove garlic, crushed

2 pounds (910 g) salmon fillets

Preheat barbecue. In a small mixing bowl, combine all ingredients except salmon. Mix well. Brush 1 side of the salmon with the basting sauce, then place the salmon (basted side down) on the grill. When the salmon is half finished cooking, baste the top portion of the salmon and carefully flip the fillet so the fresh basting sauce is on the grill. When the fish is almost finished cooking, apply the basting sauce and flip the salmon again. Baste and flip the salmon once more and serve. Be careful not to overcook the salmon as it will lose its juices and flavor if cooked too long.

**NUTRITIONAL ANALYSIS**

**EACH WITH:** 111 g water; 334 calories (45% from fat, 37% from protein, 19% from carb); 30 g protein; 16 g total fat; 3 g saturated fat; 6 g monounsaturated fat; 6 g polyunsaturated fat; 15 g carb; 0 g fiber; 15 g sugar; 28 mg calcium; 1 mg iron; 93 mg sodium; 591 mg potassium; 76 IU vitamin A; 6 mg vitamin C; 89 mg cholesterol

# Salmon Packets

Yield: 2 servings

*On hot days, it's sometimes a good idea to not use the stove at all. This recipe gives you meat and starch in one easy grilled packet.*

1 cup (195 g) instant rice

1 cup (235 ml) low sodium chicken broth

½ cup (120 g) carrot, shredded

8 ounces (225 g) salmon fillets

¼ teaspoon black pepper

½ lemon, sliced

Heat grill to medium. Spray 2 large pieces of heavy-duty aluminum foil with nonstick vegetable oil spray. In a small bowl, mix together rice and broth. Let stand until most of the broth is absorbed, about 5 minutes. Stir in the carrot. Place salmon fillet in center of each piece of foil. Sprinkle with pepper and place lemon slices on top. Place rice around fillet. Fold up foil and bring edges together. Fold over several times to seal. Fold in ends, allowing some room for rice expansion. Place on grill and grill until salmon is done, 10 to 15 minutes.

**NUTRITIONAL ANALYSIS**

**EACH WITH:** 240 g water; 414 calories (28% from fat, 28% from protein, 44% from carb); 28 g protein; 13 g total fat; 3 g saturated fat; 4 g monounsaturated fat; 5 g polyunsaturated fat; 45 g carb; 2 g fiber; 2 g sugar; 47 mg calcium; 3 mg iron; 140 mg sodium; 647 mg potassium; 3912 IU vitamin A; 15 mg vitamin C; 67 mg cholesterol

# Seafood Bundles

Yield: 4 servings

*An Italian-flavored bundle of seafood and vegetables, cooked on the grill. Serve over pasta.*

- 8 ounces (225 g) shrimp
- 16 ounces (455 g) flounder fillets, cubed
- 2 cups (360 g) tomatoes, coarsely chopped
- 1 onion, coarsely chopped
- 1 green bell pepper, coarsely chopped
- 8 ounces (225 g) mushrooms, sliced
- 2 cloves garlic
- 1½ teaspoons Italian seasoning
- ¼ cup (60 ml) white wine

Combine all ingredients except wine. Divide between 4 pieces of heavy-duty aluminum foil that have been sprayed with nonstick vegetable oil spray. Sprinkle a tablespoonful of wine over each. Fold foil up and seal on all sides. Grill over medium heat until fish is done, about 15 minutes.

### NUTRITIONAL ANALYSIS

**EACH WITH:** 332 g water; 223 calories (12% from fat, 68% from protein, 20% from carb); 36 g protein; 3 g total fat; 1 g saturated fat; 0 g monounsaturated fat; 1 g polyunsaturated fat; 11 g carb; 3 g fiber; 5 g sugar; 79 mg calcium; 3 mg iron; 185 mg sodium; 1002 mg potassium; 924 IU vitamin A; 46 mg vitamin C; 141 mg cholesterol

# Seafood Kabobs

Yield: 6 servings

*We made these for a birthday dinner for my wife's mother when she turned 92.*

- ½ pound (225 g) catfish fillets
- ½ pound (225 g) salmon fillets
- ½ cup (120 ml) olive oil
- 3 tablespoons (45 ml) lemon juice
- 1 teaspoon dried basil
- 1 tablespoon (0.4 g) dried parsley
- 1 teaspoon black pepper
- ½ pound (225 g) shrimp
- ½ pound (225 g) sea scallops

Cut catfish and salmon fillets into 1-inch (2.5-cm) cubes. Mix together oil, lemon juice, and spices. Marinate seafood in mixture 1 to 2 hours. Thread catfish, salmon, shrimp, and scallops on skewers and grill over medium coals until done, about 10 minutes.

### NUTRITIONAL ANALYSIS

**EACH WITH:** 123 g water; 358 calories (66% from fat, 31% from protein, 3% from carb); 28 g protein; 26 g total fat; 4 g saturated fat; 16 g monounsaturated fat; 4 g polyunsaturated fat; 3 g carb; 0 g fiber; 0 g sugar; 49 mg calcium; 2 mg iron; 161 mg sodium; 480 mg potassium; 244 IU vitamin A; 9 mg vitamin C; 110 mg cholesterol

### TIP

A trick to make these kinds of kabobs easier to turn: Thread 2 skewers through each piece side by side so they don't just rotate to the heavy side when you pick them up.

# Grilled Fish

Yield: 4 servings

*The original island recipe calls for Scotch bonnet pepper, one of the hottest varieties around. I used jalapeños instead and it had good flavor and acceptable heat.*

2 tablespoons (30 ml) olive oil

1 teaspoon garlic, minced

1½ tablespoons (25 ml) lime juice

1 teaspoon fresh ginger, minced

1 jalapeño pepper, seeded and sliced

1 pound (455 g) cod fillets

½ teaspoon black pepper

Combine the olive oil with the garlic, lime juice, ginger, and pepper in a mixing bowl. Add the fish fillets and turn to coat them well. Cover and refrigerate for 1 hour. Heat grill and remove the fillets from the marinade and scrape off most of the garlic and ginger pieces. Season the fish with pepper and cook over grill until done.

## NUTRITIONAL ANALYSIS

**EACH WITH:** 57 g water; 113 calories (58% from fat, 37% from protein, 5% from carb); 10 g protein; 7 g total fat; 1 g saturated fat; 5 g monounsaturated fat; 1 g polyunsaturated fat; 1 g carb; 0 g fiber; 0 g sugar; 13 mg calcium; 0 mg iron; 32 mg sodium; 265 mg potassium; 55 IU vitamin A; 4 mg vitamin C; 25 mg cholesterol

# Fish with Stewed Tomatoes

Yield: 4 servings

*Just looking for a little different way to cook fish, catfish fillets in this case, but you could use any whitefish. If you can't locate no-salt-added stewed tomatoes, you can make your own by adding a little celery, onion, and green bell pepper to plain tomatoes.*

2 cups (475 ml) no-salt-added stewed tomatoes

1 pound (455 mg) catfish fillets

½ cup (60 g) no-salt-added bread crumbs

Place tomatoes in the bottom of a 9 x 13-inch (23 x 33-cm) baking pan sprayed with nonstick vegetable oil spray. Place the fish on top. Sprinkle with bread crumbs. Bake at 350°F (180°C, gas mark 4) until fish flakes easily, about 10 to 15 minutes depending on thickness of fillets.

## NUTRITIONAL ANALYSIS

**EACH WITH:** 199 g water; 229 calories (38% from fat, 36% from protein, 26% from carb); 21 g protein; 9 g total fat; 2 g saturated fat; 4 g monounsaturated fat; 2 g polyunsaturated fat; 15 g carb; 2 g fiber; 4 g sugar; 71 mg calcium; 2 mg iron; 77 mg sodium; 638 mg potassium; 214 IU vitamin A; 18 mg vitamin C; 53 mg cholesterol

# Crabless Soup

Yield: 4 servings

*This soup is typical of Maryland crab soup in flavor. The only big difference is the lack of crabmeat, which is high in both sodium and cholesterol. In its place we have fish. I happened to have some flounder fillets available, but any whitefish would do. This is also one of our spicier recipes. You can vary the amount of extra pepper if you wish for a milder version.*

1 pound (455 g) flounder

2 cups (475 ml) low sodium chicken broth

2 cups (475 ml) no-salt-added tomatoes, diced

½ cup (65 g) frozen corn

½ cup (65 g) no-salt-added frozen peas

1½ teaspoons New Bay Seasoning, (see recipe, page 17)

½ teaspoon black pepper

½ teaspoon cayenne pepper

Shred the fish (processing in a food processor with a little of the broth does this easily). Place all ingredients in a large saucepan and simmer until fish and vegetables are cooked.

**NUTRITIONAL ANALYSIS**

**EACH WITH:** 292 g water; 105 calories (7% from fat, 44% from protein, 49% from carb); 12 g protein; 1 g total fat; 0 g saturated fat; 0 g monounsaturated fat; 0 g polyunsaturated fat; 14 g carb; 3 g fiber; 5 g sugar; 60 mg calcium; 2 mg iron; 108 mg sodium; 612 mg potassium; 733 IU vitamin A; 22 mg vitamin C; 20 mg cholesterol

# Mediterranean Fish Soup

Yield: 4 servings

*This is a soup to warm you on a cold night. A slice of bread is all that's needed to make it a meal.*

4 ounces (115 g) orzo, or other small pasta

½ cup (80 g) onion, chopped

2 cloves garlic, minced

1 teaspoon fennel seed

4 cups (940 ml) no-salt-added stewed tomatoes

2 cups (475 ml) low sodium chicken broth

1 tablespoon (0.4 g) dried parsley

½ teaspoon black pepper

¼ teaspoon turmeric

12 ounces (340 g) fish, cut into 1-inch (2.5 cm) cubes

Cook pasta according to package directions. Drain and set aside. In a large nonstick saucepan sprayed with nonstick vegetable oil spray, cook onion, garlic, and fennel seed until onion is tender. Add tomatoes, broth, and spices. Reduce heat and simmer for 10 minutes. Add fish and simmer until fish is cooked through, about 5 minutes. Divide pasta among 4 bowls. Ladle soup over pasta.

**NUTRITIONAL ANALYSIS**

**EACH WITH:** 445 g water; 192 calories (7% from fat, 46% from protein, 47% from carb); 23 g protein; 2 g total fat; 0 g saturated fat; 0 g monounsaturated fat; 0 g polyunsaturated fat; 23 g carb; 3 g fiber; 8 g sugar; 115 mg calcium; 2 mg iron; 144 mg sodium; 1020 mg potassium; 423 IU vitamin A; 39 mg vitamin C; 41 mg cholesterol

# Tuna-Rice Casserole

Yield: 4 servings

*Ever have one of those nights where you can't think of a thing for dinner and end up pawing randomly through cookbooks looking for something that sounds good and that you have the ingredients for? This was the result. And it actually worked out well. The top layer is a quiche-like custard.*

2 cups (330 g) rice, cooked

4 eggs, beaten, divided

2 tablespoons (28 g) unsalted butter, melted

½ teaspoon dried basil

1 teaspoon minced onion

1 can (6 ounces, or 170 g) low sodium tuna

1 cup (235 ml) skim milk

4 ounces (115 g) Swiss cheese, shredded

Combine rice, 1 egg, the melted butter, the basil, and the onion. Press into the bottom of an 8 x 8-inch (20 x 20-cm) baking dish sprayed with nonstick vegetable oil spray. Spread tuna over top. Combine remaining eggs, milk, and cheese and pour over top. Bake at 350°F (180°C, gas mark 4) for 40 to 45 minutes until a knife inserted near the center comes out clean.

NUTRITIONAL ANALYSIS

**EACH WITH:** 195 g water; 314 calories (36% from fat, 29% from protein, 35% from carb); 22 g protein; 12 g total fat; 6 g saturated fat; 4 g monounsaturated fat; 1 g polyunsaturated fat; 27 g carb; 1 g fiber; 1 g sugar; 147 mg calcium; 3 mg iron; 142 mg sodium; 345 mg potassium; 616 IU vitamin A; 2 mg vitamin C; 274 mg cholesterol

# Tuna-Pasta Salad–Stuffed Tomatoes

Yield: 4 servings

*A good meal for hot weather. The veggies can be varied to suit your taste. Feel free to use whatever you have on hand and/or usually use for pasta salad.*

1 can (6 ounces, or 170 g) low sodium tuna

1½ cups (75 g) pasta, cooked, drained, and cooled

2 tablespoons zucchini, chopped

2 tablespoons (12.5 g) celery, chopped

2 tablespoons (15 g) carrot, shredded

2 tablespoons (15 g) green bell pepper, chopped

2 tablespoons (17 g) cucumber, chopped

¼ cup (60 g) low sodium mayonnaise

¼ cup (60 g) sour cream

½ teaspoon celery seed

½ teaspoon onion powder

4 tomatoes

Lettuce leaves

Mix together tuna, pasta, veggies, mayonnaise, sour cream, and spices. Remove stems and hard centers from tomatoes. Cut almost through in both directions, leaving 4 wedges. Place tomatoes on lettuce on a plate, spreading them out. Pile the salad in the middle.

NUTRITIONAL ANALYSIS

**EACH WITH:** 61 g water; 237 calories (57% from fat, 23% from protein, 21% from carb); 13 g protein; 15 g total fat; 4 g saturated fat; 4 g monounsaturated fat; 6 g polyunsaturated fat; 12 g carb; 1 g fiber; 1 g sugar; 38 mg calcium; 1 mg iron; 42 mg sodium; 204 mg potassium; 682 IU vitamin A; 3 mg vitamin C; 40 mg cholesterol

# CHAPTER 10

# Soups, Stews, and Chilis

*During the winter, we have soup or chili at least twice a week. It's the sort of thing that really warms you up on a cold day. But soup also works well in warmer weather. Most of these recipes can be made in a slow cooker, allowing you to cook without heating up the kitchen. A simple soup may turn out to be just the kind of light fare you are looking for during the summer. Add to this that soups in general are nutritionally rich and low in fat and they are the kind of thing that you may want to consider having more often.*

# Beef Barley Soup

Yield: 6 servings

*This has been a family favorite for quite a while. I've also made it successfully just by dumping everything in the slow cooker.*

1 pound (455 g) ground beef

1 large onion, chopped

8 ounces (225 g) mushroom, chopped

2 cups (475 ml) low sodium chicken broth

4 cups (940 ml) water

2 teaspoons (10 ml) low sodium beef bouillon

1 cup (184 g) barley

½ teaspoon garlic powder

2 teaspoons (10 ml) Worcestershire sauce

½ teaspoon dried thyme

½ teaspoon black pepper

1 cup (120 g) carrot, shredded

Brown ground beef and onion in a large Dutch oven. When beef is almost done, add mushrooms and cook a few minutes more. Add remaining ingredients except carrot and cook until barley is done, about an hour, adding water as needed. Add carrots and cook until they are tender, about 5 minutes.

### NUTRITIONAL ANALYSIS

**EACH WITH:** 344 g water; 307 calories (30% from fat, 27% from protein, 44% from carb); 21 g protein; 10 g total fat; 4 g saturated fat; 4 g monounsaturated fat; 1 g polyunsaturated fat; 34 g carb; 7 g fiber; 3 g sugar; 43 mg calcium; 3 mg iron; 129 mg sodium; 581 mg potassium; 2594 IU vitamin A; 7 mg vitamin C; 46 mg cholesterol

# Beef Vegetable Soup

Yield: 8 servings

*Nothing fancy here, just a flavorful soup like your Grandma used to make and Campbell's wishes they could put in a can.*

1½ pounds (680 g) round steak, cut into ½-inch (1¼-cm) pieces

1 onion, coarsely chopped

½ cup (50 g) celery, sliced

4 potatoes, cubed

4 cups (940 ml) low sodium beef broth

1 cup (90 g) cabbage, coarsely chopped

4 cups (520 g) frozen mixed vegetables

2 cups (475 ml) no-salt-added tomatoes

Brown meat in a skillet and transfer to slow cooker. Add onion, celery, and potatoes. Pour broth over. Cook on low for 8 to 10 hours. Add cabbage, mixed vegetables, and tomatoes. Turn to high and cook until vegetables are done, a half hour to an hour.

### NUTRITIONAL ANALYSIS

**EACH WITH:** 443 g water; 390 calories (16% from fat, 36% from protein, 49% from carb); 35 g protein; 7 g total fat; 2 g saturated fat; 3 g monounsaturated fat; 0 g polyunsaturated fat; 47 g carb; 8 g fiber; 7 g sugar; 77 mg calcium; 5 mg iron; 144 mg sodium; 1208 mg potassium; 128 IU vitamin A; 29 mg vitamin C; 82 mg cholesterol

# Minestrone

Yield: 8 servings

*A fairly traditional vegetarian version of the classic Italian soup.*

2 tablespoons (30 ml) olive oil

1 onion, chopped

½ cup (65 g) carrot, peeled and chopped

½ cup (50 g) celery, chopped

2 cloves garlic, minced

¼ teaspoon freshly ground black pepper

2 cups (475 ml) no-salt-added tomatoes

5 cups (1175 ml) low sodium chicken broth

1 tablespoon (2.5 g) fresh basil

1 tablespoon (4 g) fresh oregano

1 tablespoon (4 g) fresh parsley

¼ pound (115 g) fresh green beans, stemmed and cut into 1-inch (2.5-cm) lengths

½ cup (100 g) great northern beans, cooked

2 cups zucchini, quartered and chopped

1 cup (150 g) shell pasta, uncooked

In a large soup pot, heat the olive oil over medium heat. Add the onion, carrot, and celery and cook for 5 minutes, or until the vegetables begin to soften. Add the garlic and pepper and cook for 2 minutes more. Add the tomatoes, chicken broth, and herbs, bring to a boil, and turn down to a simmer. Add beans and simmer for 2 minutes. Add the zucchini and pasta and simmer for 10 minutes, or until all of the vegetables are tender and the pasta is al dente.

## NUTRITIONAL ANALYSIS

**EACH WITH:** 282 g water; 138 calories (24% from fat, 18% from protein, 58% from carb); 6 g protein; 4 g total fat; 1 g saturated fat; 3 g monounsaturated fat; 1 g polyunsaturated fat; 21 g carb; 3 g fiber; 4 g sugar; 69 mg calcium; 2 mg iron; 83 mg sodium; 529 mg potassium; 1325 IU vitamin A; 20 mg vitamin C; 0 mg cholesterol

# Tomato Vegetable Soup

Yield: 4 servings

*This recipe comes from newsletter subscriber Sunshine, who started with our cream of tomato soup and created a really good veggie soup.*

1 medium onion, chopped fine

½ green bell pepper, chopped fine

2 cloves garlic, chopped fine

1 tablespoon (15 ml) vegetable oil

1 cup (235 ml) low sodium chicken broth

3½ cups (825 ml) water, divided

1 cup (150 g) macaroni

1 teaspoon low sodium beef bouillon

2 cups (475 ml) no-salt-added tomatoes

½ cup (55 g) nonfat dry milk powder

¼ teaspoon No-Salt Seasoning (see page 14)

¼ teaspoon white pepper

½ cup (65 g) frozen corn

½ cup (65 g) no-salt-added frozen peas

½ jalapeño pepper, roasted and minced

Sauté onion, bell pepper, and garlic in oil until well cooked. Combine chicken broth with enough water (about 2 cups, or 475 ml) to cook the macaroni. Bring to a boil and add macaroni. Cook for 12 minutes. Drain and store broth for other uses. Puree the bouillon, tomatoes, dry milk, seasonings, the remaining 1½ cups (355 ml) water, and sautéed onion, bell pepper, and garlic. Combine pureed sauce, macaroni, corn, peas, and minced jalapeño and simmer for a half hour.

## NUTRITIONAL ANALYSIS

**EACH WITH:** 361 g water; 162 calories (4% from fat, 21% from protein, 75% from carb); 9 g protein; 1 g total fat; 0 g saturated fat; 0 g monounsaturated fat; 0 g polyunsaturated fat; 32 g carb; 4 g fiber; 12 g sugar; 167 mg calcium; 2 mg iron; 109 mg sodium; 648 mg potassium; 912 IU vitamin A; 39 mg vitamin C; 2 mg cholesterol

# Black Bean Soup

Yield: 6 servings

*A flavorful Latin-style soup that's low in fat. Use homemade salsa if you have it. If not, look for a brand like Enrico's no salt added, which is just as low, or Newman's Own, which has around 120 mg of sodium per serving. That will add about 30 mg per serving.*

1½ cups (250 g) dried black beans

4 cups (940 ml) water

1 onion, finely chopped

½ green bell pepper, finely chopped

2 cloves garlic, minced

1 cup (130 g) carrot, finely chopped

½ cup (50 g) celery, finely chopped

2 tablespoons (28 ml) olive oil

1 teaspoon cumin

¼ teaspoon cayenne pepper

1 tablespoon (15 ml) lime juice

¼ cup (56 g) salsa

Soak beans in water overnight. In a large Dutch oven, sauté onion, bell pepper, garlic, carrot, and celery in oil until almost soft. Add spices and sauté a few minutes more. Add beans, water, lime juice, and salsa and simmer until beans are beginning to fall apart, 1½ to 2 hours.

**NUTRITIONAL ANALYSIS**

**EACH WITH:** 257 g water; 124 calories (34% from fat, 14% from protein, 51% from carb); 5 g protein; 5 g total fat; 1 g saturated fat; 3 g monounsaturated fat; 1 g polyunsaturated fat; 17 g carb; 5 g fiber; 3 g sugar; 40 mg calcium; 1 mg iron; 32 mg sodium; 335 mg potassium; 2770 IU vitamin A; 15 mg vitamin C; 0 mg cholesterol

# Southwestern Bean Soup

Yield: 8 servings

*One Sunday, I was looking for a fairly large pot of some kind of soup to use for lunches for the week. My original idea was chili, but I had lots of navy beans and no kidney or pinto ones, so this is what we came up with. This is a vegetarian version, but you could add some chicken to it if you're the kind who has to have real meat. This makes a moderately spicy soup, but you can also adjust the heat to your desire by using more or less pepper.*

1½ cups (375 g) navy beans

6 cups (1410 ml) water

½ chipotle pepper

½ onion, chopped

½ teaspoon garlic powder

1½ teaspoons cumin

2 cups (475 ml) no-salt-added tomatoes, chopped

6 ounces (170 g) frozen corn

8 ounces (230 g) orzo, or other small pasta

Soak beans in water overnight or bring to boil, boil 1 minute, and let stand 1 hour. Add pepper, onion, and spices and simmer until beans are almost tender, 1 to 1½ hours. Add tomatoes, corn, and pasta and cook until pasta and beans are done. Remove pepper before serving.

**NUTRITIONAL ANALYSIS**

**EACH WITH:** 265 g water; 274 calories (5% from fat, 20% from protein, 76% from carb); 14 g protein; 1 g total fat; 0 g saturated fat; 0 g monounsaturated fat; 1 g polyunsaturated fat; 53 g carb; 12 g fiber; 4 g sugar; 93 mg calcium; 4 mg iron; 22 mg sodium; 729 mg potassium; 345 IU vitamin A; 12 mg vitamin C; 0 mg cholesterol

# Amish Chicken Corn Soup

Yield: 8 servings

*This is similar to the Amish chicken corn soup that was often served at volunteer fire company carnivals and suppers in the south central Pennsylvania/north central Maryland area where I grew up. My mother always added a can of baked beans to hers, but I've decided not to go with that here.*

4 cups (940 ml) low sodium chicken broth

2 cups (220 g) chicken, cooked and chopped

½ cup (50 g) celery, chopped

½ cup (65 g) carrot, sliced

12 ounces (340 g) frozen corn

1 onion, chopped

1 tablespoon (0.4 g) dried parsley

¼ teaspoon garlic powder

2 cups (475 ml) water

12 ounces egg noodles

Place all ingredients in a large kettle and simmer until noodles and corn are tender.

**NUTRITIONAL ANALYSIS**

**EACH WITH:** 288 g water; 178 calories (18% from fat, 34% from protein, 48% from carb); 16 g protein; 4 g total fat; 1 g saturated fat; 1 g monounsaturated fat; 1 g polyunsaturated fat; 22 g carb; 2 g fiber; 3 g sugar; 29 mg calcium; 2 mg iron; 100 mg sodium; 383 mg potassium; 1152 IU vitamin A; 6 mg vitamin C; 45 mg cholesterol

# French Onion Soup

Yield: 4 servings

*My daughter wanted some onion soup, so she started digging for recipes. (Actually, as soon as she mentioned it I realized how long it had been since I'd had any.) We came up with this recipe, which is a variation of one in a* Better Homes and Gardens *vegetable cookbook.*

1 pound (455 g) onions, sliced

2 tablespoons (28 g) unsalted butter

4 cups (940 ml) low sodium beef broth

1 tablespoon (15 ml) Worcestershire sauce

4 slices low sodium French bread

2 slices Swiss cheese

In a heavy, covered saucepan, cook onions in butter at low temperature until soft, 15 to 20 minutes. Add broth and Worcestershire sauce and bring to boiling. Lightly toast bread under broiler. Place ½ slice of cheese on each piece of bread and broil until bubbly. Float a slice of bread on each bowl of soup.

**NUTRITIONAL ANALYSIS**

**EACH WITH:** 248 g water; 222 calories (27% from fat, 19% from protein, 54% from carb); 10 g protein; 7 g total fat; 4 g saturated fat; 2 g monounsaturated fat; 1 g polyunsaturated fat; 30 g carb; 3 g fiber; 5 g sugar; 61 mg calcium; 2 mg iron; 110 mg sodium; 397 mg potassium; 181 IU vitamin A; 11 mg vitamin C; 15 mg cholesterol

# Potato and Corn Chowder

Yield: 6 servings

*This is great just the way it is or you can add some cooked chicken or ground turkey if you like. We like it just like this with breadsticks and nothing else.*

4 tablespoons (55 g) unsalted butter

1 onion, chopped

½ cup (50 g) celery, sliced

½ cup (65 g) carrot, sliced

2 tablespoons (16 g) all-purpose flour

2 cups (475 ml) low sodium chicken broth

4 cups (940 ml) skim milk

2 potatoes, peeled and diced

3 cups (390 g) frozen white corn

½ teaspoon black pepper

Melt the butter in a large Dutch oven. Add the onion, celery, and carrots and cook over medium heat until just soft. Sprinkle on the flour and cook for 3 minutes, stirring frequently. Stir in the broth and milk. Add the potatoes and corn. Simmer for 25 minutes or until potatoes are tender.

## NUTRITIONAL ANALYSIS

**EACH WITH:** 371 g water; 275 calories (27% from fat, 16% from protein, 57% from carb); 12 g protein; 9 g total fat; 5 g saturated fat; 2 g monounsaturated fat; 1 g polyunsaturated fat; 41 g carb; 4 g fiber; 4 g sugar; 267 mg calcium; 1 mg iron; 152 mg sodium; 820 mg potassium; 1902 IU vitamin A; 18 mg vitamin C; 24 mg cholesterol

# Seafood Chowder

Yield: 6 servings

*This one came about on a weekend when I didn't want to spend my day cooking and I knew everyone was going to be available for dinner at a different time. The answer . . . the slow cooker and a fish and shrimp soup that people could ladle up whenever they were ready.*

½ pound (225 g) cod or other whitefish, cubed

½ pound (225 g) shrimp, peeled

4 potatoes, shredded

1 cup (120 g) carrots, shredded

½ onion, finely chopped

½ cup (60 g) red bell pepper, finely chopped

½ cup (60 g) celery, finely chopped

2 cups (475 ml) water

1 teaspoon low sodium chicken bouillon

1 cup (235 ml) skim milk

1 teaspoon New Bay Seasoning (see recipe, page 17)

Place fish and shrimp in slow cooker. Add vegetables. Combine water and bouillon powder. Pour over meat and vegetables. Add milk and seasoning. Stir to mix. Cook on low for 8 to 10 hours.

## NUTRITIONAL ANALYSIS

**EACH WITH:** 379 g water; 276 calories (4% from fat, 29% from protein, 67% from carb); 20 g protein; 1 g total fat; 0 g saturated fat; 0 g monounsaturated fat; 0 g polyunsaturated fat; 47 g carb; 5 g fiber; 4 g sugar; 112 mg calcium; 2 mg iron; 205 mg sodium; 1101 mg potassium; 3217 IU vitamin A; 43 mg vitamin C; 91 mg cholesterol

# Cream of Tomato Soup

Yield: **3 servings**

*This isn't exactly your traditional cream of tomato soup. I really wanted something warm, but more substantial than just a cup of tea or coffee. This makes about 3 mugs full of a soup that can be heated in the microwave and sipped on to warm you and fill you at the same time.*

- 1 teaspoon sodium-free beef bouillon
- 2 cups (475 ml) no-salt-added tomatoes
- ¼ cup (28 g) nonfat dry milk powder
- 1 teaspoon No-Salt Seasoning (see recipe, page 14)
- ¼ teaspoon white pepper
- 1 cup (235 ml) water

Combine all ingredients in a blender container. Blend until tomatoes are well pureed. Heat and sip.

**NUTRITIONAL ANALYSIS**

**EACH WITH:** 229 g water; 52 calories (4% from fat, 24% from protein, 72% from carb); 4 g protein; 0 g total fat; 0 g saturated fat; 0 g monounsaturated fat; 0 g polyunsaturated fat; 10 g carb; 2 g fiber; 8 g sugar; 120 mg calcium; 1 mg iron; 76 mg sodium; 468 mg potassium; 361 IU vitamin A; 23 mg vitamin C; 1 mg cholesterol

# Classic Beef Stew

Yield: **8 servings**

*This was a suggestion from my daughter, who recently made her annual pilgrimage to Maryland's Renaissance Festival but missed out on her usual walk-about meal of beef stew in a bread bowl. This makes a big batch, but you could halve the quantities if desired.*

- 2 cups (475 ml) low sodium beef broth
- 2 cups (475 ml) no-salt-added stewed tomatoes
- ½ teaspoon garlic powder
- ½ teaspoon black pepper
- 1 tablespoon (0.4 g) dried parsley
- 2 pounds (910 g) beef chuck, trimmed and cubed
- 2½ cups (295 g) carrots, peeled and sliced
- 1 onion, quartered
- 1 pound (455 g) pasta

Mix broth, tomatoes, and spices. Place beef and veggies in large roasting pan. Pour broth mixture over. Roast, covered, at 325°F (170°C, gas mark 3) until meat is very tender, 2 to 2½ hours. Serve over pasta.

**NUTRITIONAL ANALYSIS**

**EACH WITH:** 180 g water; 533 calories (42% from fat, 22% from protein, 37% from carb); 29 g protein; 25 g total fat; 9 g saturated fat; 10 g monounsaturated fat; 2 g polyunsaturated fat; 49 g carb; 4 g fiber; 5 g sugar; 65 mg calcium; 4 mg iron; 123 mg sodium; 732 mg potassium; 4968 IU vitamin A; 13 mg vitamin C; 134 mg cholesterol

# Cider Stew

Yield: 8 servings

*I came across this recipe while looking for slow cooker recipes; however, the sodium level was much too high, so I tweaked it until there was nothing that doesn't work well for someone watching their sodium.*

2 pounds (910 g) beef stew meat, cubed

2 tablespoons (28 ml) vegetable oil

3 tablespoons (24 g) all-purpose flour

¼ teaspoon dried thyme

¼ teaspoon black pepper

1 cup (130 g) carrot, sliced

3 medium potatoes, chopped

2 onions, sliced

¼ cup (25 g) celery, sliced

1 apple, chopped

1 tablespoon (15 ml) vinegar

2 cups (475 ml) apple cider

2 tablespoons (16 g) cornstarch

½ cup (120 ml) cold water

In a skillet, brown half the meat at a time in a tablespoon of oil. Combine flour, thyme, and pepper. Toss with browned meat to coat. Place vegetables and apple in slow cooker. Place meat on top. Mix together vinegar and cider. Pour over meat and vegetables. Cook on low for 8 to 10 hours or on high for 5 to 6 hours. Turn heat to high. Stir cornstarch into water. Add to slow cooker. Cook until sauce is thickened, 15 to 20 minutes, and serve.

### NUTRITIONAL ANALYSIS

**EACH WITH:** 277 g water; 520 calories (40% from fat, 28% from protein, 32% from carb); 36 g protein; 23 g total fat; 8 g saturated fat; 9 g monounsaturated fat; 3 g polyunsaturated fat; 41 g carb; 3 g fiber; 12 g sugar; 41 mg calcium; 5 mg iron; 93 mg sodium; 866 mg potassium; 1955 IU vitamin A; 13 mg vitamin C; 113 mg cholesterol

# Black Bean Turkey Chili

Yield: 6 servings

*This makes a rather mild chili, but you can easily add more chili powder or some red pepper flakes to spice it up.*

1 pound (455 g) turkey, ground

1 tablespoon (15 ml) olive oil

½ onion, chopped

½ green bell pepper, seeded and chopped

2 cloves garlic, minced

4 cups (900 g) no-salt-added black beans, rinsed and drained

2 cups (475 ml) no-salt-added stewed tomatoes

8 ounces (230 g) no-salt-added tomato sauce

1 cup (235 ml) dark beer or low sodium beef broth

1 tablespoon (7.5 g) chili powder

1 tablespoon (7 g) ground cumin

1 teaspoon ground coriander

1 teaspoon dried oregano, crushed

Heat large heavy saucepan or Dutch oven to medium high. Brown the meat until cooked, then drain and set aside. In the skillet, heat the oil, then add the onion, bell pepper, and garlic, and cook until tender, 5 to 6 minutes. Return meat to pan. Add remaining ingredients. Bring chili to a boil; then reduce heat and simmer for 30 to 45 minutes or until thickened, stirring occasionally.

### NUTRITIONAL ANALYSIS

**EACH WITH:** 259 g water; 350 calories (18% from fat, 40% from protein, 42% from carb); 35 g protein; 7 g total fat; 2 g saturated fat; 3 g monounsaturated fat; 2 g polyunsaturated fat; 36 g carb; 14 g fiber; 3 g sugar; 126 mg calcium; 5 mg iron; 71 mg sodium; 962 mg potassium; 552 IU vitamin A; 24 mg vitamin C; 58 mg cholesterol

# Chili con Carne

Yield: 8 servings

*This makes a nice thick, moderately spicy chili. The preparation isn't difficult, but like most chili it's best if it's simmered for a while.*

2 pounds (910 g) ground beef

1 tablespoon (15 ml) olive oil

1 medium onion, chopped

1 cup (120 g) red bell pepper, chopped

½ teaspoon garlic, minced

½ teaspoon black pepper, freshly ground

1 teaspoon ground cumin

1 ounce (28 g) dried chipotle pepper, ground

1 teaspoon cayenne pepper

1 tablespoon (7.5 g) chili powder

3 cups (705 ml) water

6 ounces (170 g) no-salt-added tomato paste

4 cups (940 ml) no-salt-added tomatoes

4 cups (900 g) no-salt-added kidney beans

Brown beef in 2 batches in thick-bottomed soup kettle. Drain off fat and set browned beef aside. Heat oil in kettle over medium-high heat, adding onion when hot. Sauté for 4 to 5 minutes, stirring often. Add bell pepper and garlic, continuing to cook for 2 to 3 more minutes. Add black pepper, ground cumin, chipotle, and cayenne to taste plus chili powder. Stir continually until spices begin to stick to bottom of kettle and brown. Quickly add the water. Add tomato paste and tomatoes with the juice they were packed in. Add the kidney beans. Add the beef, but try not to include any fat that may have accumulated. Stir. When chili begins to boil, reduce heat to low and cover. Ideally chili should be simmered for 3 hours to let all the flavors blend together. Stir about every 15 minutes, while checking to make sure the heat is not too high, causing the chili to stick to the bottom of the kettle. If you don't have 3 hours to cook the chili, use less chipotle and cayenne or else they will overpower the other flavors.

**NUTRITIONAL ANALYSIS**

**EACH WITH:** 364 g water; 478 calories (39% from fat, 32% from protein, 28% from carb); 39 g protein; 21 g total fat; 8 g saturated fat; 10 g monounsaturated fat; 1 g polyunsaturated fat; 34 g carb; 12 g fiber; 7 g sugar; 124 mg calcium; 7 mg iron; 122 mg sodium; 1369 mg potassium; 1871 IU vitamin A; 42 mg vitamin C; 92 mg cholesterol

# Chicken and Barley Chili

Yield: 9 servings

*Okay, it's not like any chili you've had before. But the flavor is fantastic, one of those dishes that no one will even recognize as being low sodium. If you can't find the quick-cooking variety of barley, as I often can't, you'll have to use the long-cooking kind and precook it.*

1 cup (160 g) onion, chopped

1 clove garlic, minced

1 tablespoon (15 ml) vegetable oil

2 cups (475 ml) water

¾ cup (138 g) barley, quick cooking

4 cups (940 ml) no-salt-added tomatoes

2 cups (475 ml) low sodium chicken broth

6 ounces (170 g) frozen corn

1 can (4 ounces, or 115 g) jalapeños, chopped

1 tablespoon (7.5 g) chili powder

½ tablespoon cumin

3 cups (330 g) chicken, cooked and cubed

In a Dutch oven, cook the onion and garlic in the oil until the onion is tender. Add all the remaining ingredients except the chicken. Bring to a boil. Reduce the heat, cover, and simmer for 10 minutes, stirring occasionally. Add the chicken and continue simmering an additional 5 to 10 minutes until the chicken is heated through and barley is tender.

### NUTRITIONAL ANALYSIS

**EACH WITH:** 269 g water; 202 calories (23% from fat, 31% from protein, 46% from carb); 16 g protein; 5 g total fat; 1 g saturated fat; 2 g monounsaturated fat; 2 g polyunsaturated fat; 24 g carb; 5 g fiber; 5 g sugar; 56 mg calcium; 2 mg iron; 74 mg sodium; 540 mg potassium; 463 IU vitamin A; 19 mg vitamin C; 35 mg cholesterol

# White Chili

Yield: 8 servings

*This is a variation of a chili recipe that took second place at the Virginia State Fair.*

1 pound (455 g) boneless chicken breast, cubed

1 medium onion

1½ teaspoons garlic powder

1 tablespoon (15 ml) vegetable oil

4 cups (900 g) no-salt-added great northern beans

2 cups (475 ml) low sodium chicken broth

4 ounces (115 g) chopped chile peppers

1 teaspoon ground cumin

1 teaspoon dried oregano

½ teaspoon black pepper

¼ teaspoon cayenne pepper

1 cup (230 g) sour cream

In a large saucepan, sauté chicken, onion, and garlic powder in oil until chicken is no longer pink. Add beans, broth, chiles, and seasonings. Bring to a boil. Reduce heat; simmer uncovered for 30 minutes. Remove from heat; stir in sour cream.

### NUTRITIONAL ANALYSIS

**EACH WITH:** 207 g water; 269 calories (30% from fat, 34% from protein, 36% from carb); 23 g protein; 9 g total fat; 4 g saturated fat; 2 g monounsaturated fat; 2 g polyunsaturated fat; 25 g carb; 6 g fiber; 1 g sugar; 87 mg calcium; 3 mg iron; 99 mg sodium; 660 mg potassium; 474 IU vitamin A; 5 mg vitamin C; 46 mg cholesterol

# Cincinnati Chili

Yield: 6 servings

*Cincinnati, Ohio, claims to be the chili capital of the United States, with more than 180 chili parlors. Cincinnati-style chili is quite different from its more familiar Texas cousin. The chili is thinner and contains an unusual blend of spices that includes cinnamon, chocolate or cocoa, allspice, and Worcestershire.*

1 onion, chopped

1 pound (455 g) lean ground beef

¼ teaspoon garlic, minced

1 tablespoon (7.5 g) chili powder

1 teaspoon ground allspice

1 teaspoon ground cinnamon

1 teaspoon ground cumin

½ teaspoon cayenne pepper

1½ tablespoons (12 g) unsweetened cocoa powder

15 ounces (425 g) no-salt-added tomato sauce

1 tablespoon (15 ml) Worcestershire sauce

1 tablespoon (15 ml) cider vinegar

½ cup (120 ml) water

In a large frying pan over medium-high heat, sauté onion, ground beef, garlic, and chili powder until ground beef is slightly cooked. Add allspice, cinnamon, cumin, cayenne pepper, unsweetened cocoa, tomato sauce, Worcestershire sauce, cider vinegar, and water. Reduce heat to low and simmer, uncovered, for 1½ hours.

**NUTRITIONAL ANALYSIS**

**EACH WITH:** 136 g water; 193 calories (45% from fat, 32% from protein, 23% from carb); 16 g protein; 10 g total fat; 4 g saturated fat; 4 g monounsaturated fat; 1 g polyunsaturated fat; 11 g carb; 3 g fiber; 5 g sugar; 37 mg calcium; 4 mg iron; 57 mg sodium; 599 mg potassium; 804 IU vitamin A; 15 mg vitamin C; 47 mg cholesterol

**TIP**

To serve the traditional Cincinnati way, ladle chili over cooked spaghetti and serve with toppings of your choice. Two-Way Chili: Served on spaghetti. Three-Way Chili: Additionally topped with shredded cheddar cheese. Four-Way Chili: Additionally topped with chopped onion. Five-Way Chili: Additionally topped with kidney beans

CHAPTER 11

# Salads and Salad Dressings

---

*Salad dressing is often one of the more difficult things to find in low sodium versions. I've seen a couple here locally, but quite honestly, the taste wasn't anything to write home about. The best seem to be fruit-flavored and vinaigrette ones, and that just doesn't go with everything. However, all is not lost. We have in this chapter an assortment of dressings that are low in sodium but also taste good. Some are almost sodium-free. Others may contain 30 to 40 mg per 2-tablespoon (28-ml) serving, but that is much less than commercial ones and something almost anyone can work into their diet. We also have some salad ideas to put the dressings on, including some meal-size ones. And to finish the chapter off there are delicious recipes for coleslaw, potato, pasta, and other side-dish salads.*

# Blue Cheese Dressing

Yield: 20 servings

*This was the winner from my long-term experimenting. It is the best reasonably low sodium recipe for blue cheese dressing I've found so far. The key seems to be the use of "real" blue cheese for flavor, and that is where the majority of the sodium comes from. I found blue cheese with sodium content from 310 mg per ounce to well over 400 mg per ounce.*

2 ounces (55 g) blue cheese
1 cup (225 g) low sodium mayonnaise
½ cup (115 g) sour cream
½ cup (120 ml) low sodium buttermilk
Combine ingredients and chill overnight.

### NUTRITIONAL ANALYSIS

**EACH WITH:** 13 g water; 104 calories (92% from fat, 4% from protein, 3% from carb); 1 g protein; 11 g total fat; 3 g saturated fat; 3 g monounsaturated fat; 4 g polyunsaturated fat; 1 g carb; 0 g fiber; 0 g sugar; 31 mg calcium; 0 mg iron; 43 mg sodium; 29 mg potassium; 91 IU vitamin A; 0 mg vitamin C; 11 mg cholesterol

# Caesar Salad Dressing

Yield: 6 servings

*A quick and easy way to a Caesar salad taste. This eliminates some of the traditional ingredients like coddled eggs and anchovies without detracting from the flavor of the finished product.*

½ cup (120 ml) olive oil
1 clove garlic, minced
1 tablespoon (15 ml) lemon juice
2 tablespoons (30 ml) red wine vinegar
½ teaspoon Worcestershire sauce

Mix together dressing ingredients. Shake well in a jar with a tight-fitting lid.

### NUTRITIONAL ANALYSIS

**EACH WITH:** 7 g water; 161 calories (98% from fat, 0% from protein, 2% from carb); 0 g protein; 18 g total fat; 2 g saturated fat; 13 g monounsaturated fat; 2 g polyunsaturated fat; 1 g carb; 0 g fiber; 0 g sugar; 2 mg calcium; 0 mg iron; 2 mg sodium; 14 mg potassium; 1 IU vitamin A; 2 mg vitamin C; 0 mg cholesterol

# Italian Dressing

Yield: 6 servings

*A simple Italian vinaigrette dressing.*

¼ cup (60 ml) vegetable oil

½ cup (120 ml) cider vinegar

2 tablespoons (30 g) Dijon mustard

½ teaspoon garlic powder

½ teaspoon black pepper

½ teaspoon sugar

1 teaspoon dried basil

1 teaspoon dried oregano

½ teaspoon dried rosemary

Combine all ingredients in a jar with a tight-fitting lid. Shake well.

### NUTRITIONAL ANALYSIS

**EACH WITH:** 23 g water; 90 calories (89% from fat, 1% from protein, 10% from carb); 0 g protein; 9 g total fat; 1 g saturated fat; 2 g monounsaturated fat; 5 g polyunsaturated fat; 2 g carb; 0 g fiber; 2 g sugar; 12 mg calcium; 0 mg iron; 7 mg sodium; 40 mg potassium; 31 IU vitamin A; 0 mg vitamin C; 0 mg cholesterol

### TIP

A nice addition to this is a couple of tablespoons of chopped sun-dried tomatoes.

# Creamy Italian Dressing

Yield: 10 servings

*This is not only good as a salad dressing, but does very nicely for pasta salad.*

½ cup (115 g) low sodium mayonnaise

½ cup (115 g) sour cream

1 tablespoon (15 ml) olive oil

2 tablespoons (28 ml) cider vinegar

1 tablespoon (7 g) Italian seasoning

1 teaspoon dried basil

½ teaspoon garlic powder

½ teaspoon black pepper

Combine all ingredients. Store in a covered container in the refrigerator.

### NUTRITIONAL ANALYSIS

**EACH WITH:** 13 g water; 118 calories (94% from fat, 2% from protein, 5% from carb); 1 g protein; 13 g total fat; 3 g saturated fat; 4 g monounsaturated fat; 4 g polyunsaturated fat; 1 g carb; 0 g fiber; 0 g sugar; 22 mg calcium; 0 mg iron; 10 mg sodium; 34 mg potassium; 133 IU vitamin A; 0 mg vitamin C; 12 mg cholesterol

# Ranch Dressing

Yield: 12 servings

*This dressing is better if you make it ahead of time and let it sit at least overnight so the herbs soften and the flavor develops.*

½ cup (120 ml) buttermilk

1 cup (225 g) low sodium mayonnaise

1 teaspoon onion powder

1 teaspoon dried parsley

1½ teaspoons (6 g) sugar

½ teaspoon garlic powder

½ teaspoon dry mustard

¼ teaspoon dried thyme

¼ teaspoon dried basil

¼ teaspoon dried oregano

¼ teaspoon dried rosemary

¼ teaspoon dried sage

¼ teaspoon black pepper, freshly ground

Mix all the ingredients together. Store in the refrigerator in a tightly covered jar.

**NUTRITIONAL ANALYSIS**

**EACH WITH:** 13 g water; 139 calories (93% from fat, 2% from protein, 5% from carb); 1 g protein; 15 g total fat; 2 g saturated fat; 4 g monounsaturated fat; 7 g polyunsaturated fat; 2 g carb; 0 g fiber; 1 g sugar; 18 mg calcium; 0 mg iron; 17 mg sodium; 27 mg potassium; 68 IU vitamin A; 0 mg vitamin C; 11 mg cholesterol

# Honey-Mustard Dressing

Yield: 10 servings

*Honey mustard generally has less sodium than regular mustard.*

½ cup (115 g) low sodium mayonnaise

½ cup (115 g) sour cream

2 tablespoons (30 g) honey mustard

1 tablespoon (20 g) honey

1 tablespoon (15 ml) cider vinegar

½ teaspoon onion powder

¼ teaspoon garlic powder

Combine all ingredients. Store in a covered container in the refrigerator.

**NUTRITIONAL ANALYSIS**

**EACH WITH:** 14 g water; 111 calories (88% from fat, 2% from protein, 10% from carb); 1 g protein; 11 g total fat; 3 g saturated fat; 3 g monounsaturated fat; 4 g polyunsaturated fat; 3 g carb; 0 g fiber; 2 g sugar; 16 mg calcium; 0 mg iron; 27 mg sodium; 28 mg potassium; 152 IU vitamin A; 0 mg vitamin C; 12 mg cholesterol

**TIP**

This can also be used to brush on fish or chicken when grilling. If you have a local deli that carries Boar's Head deli meats and products, they make a nice honey mustard with 15 mg sodium per teaspoon.

# Coleslaw

Yield: 6 servings

*This makes a fairly sour slaw, which is just fine with me, especially if you are planning to put it on barbecue sandwiches. You could add more sugar or a little honey if you like it sweeter.*

¼ cup (60 g) low sodium mayonnaise

¼ cup (60 g) sour cream

2 tablespoons (25 ml) vinegar

2 tablespoons (26 g) sugar

¼ teaspoon celery seed

¼ teaspoon onion powder

2 cups (140 g) cabbage, shredded

⅓ cup (40 g) carrot, shredded

Stir dressing ingredients together. Pour over cabbage and carrot and stir to mix.

---

**NUTRITIONAL ANALYSIS**

**EACH WITH:** 41 g water; 112 calories (73% from fat, 3% from protein, 25% from carb); 1 g protein; 9 g total fat; 2 g saturated fat; 3 g monounsaturated fat; 4 g polyunsaturated fat; 7 g carb; 1 g fiber; 5 g sugar; 28 mg calcium; 0 mg iron; 17 mg sodium; 104 mg potassium; 973 IU vitamin A; 12 mg vitamin C; 10 mg cholesterol

# Apple-Cabbage Slaw

Yield: 8 servings

*Another little different variation on the coleslaw theme. Good with pork or chicken.*

2 tablespoons (28 g) low sodium mayonnaise

2 tablespoons (15 g) plain low-fat yogurt

½ tablespoon lemon juice

1 tablespoon (20 g) honey

¼ teaspoon celery seed

⅛ teaspoon pepper

2 cups (140 g) cabbage, shredded

1½ cups (225 g) apple, chopped

Mix together all dressing ingredients and toss with cabbage and apples.

---

**NUTRITIONAL ANALYSIS**

**EACH WITH:** 87 g water; 78 calories (31% from fat, 3% from protein, 66% from carb); 1 g protein; 3 g total fat; 0 g saturated fat; 1 g monounsaturated fat; 1 g polyunsaturated fat; 14 g carb; 1 g fiber; 11 g sugar; 19 mg calcium; 0 mg iron; 6 mg sodium; 123 mg potassium; 62 IU vitamin A; 12 mg vitamin C; 2 mg cholesterol

# Chicken Caesar Salad

Yield: **4 servings**

*One of those meal-on-a-plate type things that is good for a Friday night when you don't want to think too much about cooking.*

- 1 pound (455 g) boneless chicken breast
- 12 ounces (340 g) romaine lettuce
- ¼ cup (25 g) Parmesan cheese, grated
- ¼ teaspoon black pepper, freshly ground
- 1 cup Croutons (see recipe, page 40)

FOR DRESSING:
- ½ cup (120 ml) olive oil
- 1 clove garlic, minced
- 1 tablespoon (15 ml) lemon juice
- 2 tablespoons (30 ml) red wine vinegar
- ½ teaspoon Worcestershire sauce

Mix together dressing ingredients. Shake well in a jar with a tight-fitting lid. Place half of dressing in a resealable plastic bag with chicken breast and marinate several hours. Remove and discard dressing. Grill chicken until done. Slice into strips. Place lettuce on plates. Place chicken on top. Add croutons; sprinkle with cheese and pepper. Serve with remaining dressing.

**NUTRITIONAL ANALYSIS**

**EACH WITH:** 171 g water; 501 calories (60% from fat, 32% from protein, 8% from carb); 40 g protein; 34 g total fat; 6 g saturated fat; 22 g monounsaturated fat; 4 g polyunsaturated fat; 10 g carb; 2 g fiber; 2 g sugar; 129 mg calcium; 3 mg iron; 193 mg sodium; 544 mg potassium; 4991 IU vitamin A; 24 mg vitamin C; 102 mg cholesterol

# Chicken Chef's Salad

Yield: **2 servings**

*A quick, light main-dish salad. Good with just about any dressing, but I particularly like it with peppercorn ranch.*

- 4 cups mixed salad greens
- ¼ cup (33 g) carrot, sliced
- 1 cup (180 g) tomato, cut in wedges
- ¼ cup (30 g) red bell pepper, sliced
- 4 ounces (115 g) mushrooms, sliced
- 4 ounces (115 g) chicken breast, cooked and sliced
- 4 ounces (115 g) Swiss cheese, cut into strips
- 2 eggs, hard boiled and sliced

Layer the veggies and other ingredients in about the order described. Apply dressing and eat.

**NUTRITIONAL ANALYSIS**

**EACH WITH:** 354 g water; 446 calories (48% from fat, 40% from protein, 12% from carb); 45 g protein; 24 g total fat; 13 g saturated fat; 7 g monounsaturated fat; 2 g polyunsaturated fat; 13 g carb; 5 g fiber; 7 g sugar; 636 mg calcium; 3 mg iron; 157 mg sodium; 988 mg potassium; 3096 IU vitamin A; 56 mg vitamin C; 346 mg cholesterol

# Asian Chicken Salad

Yield: **4 servings**

*Another salad with leftover chicken, this time with an Asian influence.*

2 cups (220 g) cooked chicken, diced

6 cups (120 g) iceberg lettuce, torn into bite-size pieces

¼ cup (40 g) green onions, sliced

½ cup (30 g) cilantro, chopped

½ cup (30 g) fresh parsley, chopped

½ cup (50 g) celery, sliced

¼ cup (31 g) slivered almonds

½ cup (75 g) mandarin oranges

FOR DRESSING:

¼ cup (60 ml) rice vinegar

¼ cup sesame oil (60 ml)

¼ cup (60 ml) Soy Sauce Substitute (see recipe, page 28)

1 tablespoon (8 g) sesame seeds

For dressing, combine vinegar, oil, soy sauce, and sesame seeds. Marinate the chopped chicken in the dressing for a few hours or overnight. Toss together lettuce, onion, cilantro, parsley, and celery. Just before serving, add almonds, oranges, and chicken with dressing to salad. Toss well.

### NUTRITIONAL ANALYSIS

**EACH WITH:** 201 g water; 302 calories (63% from fat, 26% from protein, 11% from carb); 20 g protein; 21 g total fat; 3 g saturated fat; 9 g monounsaturated fat; 8 g polyunsaturated fat; 8 g carb; 3 g fiber; 6 g sugar; 69 mg calcium; 2 mg iron; 82 mg sodium; 512 mg potassium; 1674 IU vitamin A; 28 mg vitamin C; 53 mg cholesterol

# Strawberry Spinach Salad

Yield: **6 servings**

*This different kind of salad recipe comes from one of my wife's coworkers. It is a request for every luncheon and get-together they have, and it's easy to understand why.*

½ pound (225 g) spinach

½ pound (225 g) strawberries, hulled and halved

¼ red onion, sliced

¼ cucumber, sliced

⅓ cup (38 g) sliced almonds

FOR DRESSING:

1 lemon

2 tablespoons (28 ml) white wine vinegar

1 tablespoon (15 ml) vegetable oil

⅓ cup (67 g) sugar

Prepare fruit and veggies for salad. Zest the lemon. Squeeze juice into bowl. Mix with other dressing ingredients. Toss salad and dressing just before serving.

### NUTRITIONAL ANALYSIS

**EACH WITH:** 98 g water; 142 calories (39% from fat, 10% from protein, 51% from carb); 4 g protein; 7 g total fat; 1 g saturated fat; 3 g monounsaturated fat; 2 g polyunsaturated fat; 20 g carb; 3 g fiber; 15 g sugar; 87 mg calcium; 1 mg iron; 40 mg sodium; 272 mg potassium; 4580 IU vitamin A; 29 mg vitamin C; 0 mg cholesterol

# Three-Bean Salad

Yield: 6 servings

*A fairly traditional three-bean salad. Use either low sodium canned kidney beans or cook the dry ones ahead of time. You can vary the flavor by using red wine vinegar and different sweeteners.*

½ cup (120 ml) cider vinegar

¼ cup (50 g) sugar

¼ cup (60 ml) vegetable oil

¼ teaspoon garlic powder

¼ teaspoon black pepper

12 ounces (340 g) frozen green beans

12 ounces (340 g) frozen yellow beans

¼ cup (40 g) onion, diced

¼ cup (30 g) green bell pepper, diced

1 cup (100 g) kidney beans

Combine vinegar, sugar, oil, and spices. Heat until sugar melts. Cook frozen beans with onion and bell pepper until just tender. Combine marinade and vegetables and stir to mix. Refrigerate overnight.

## NUTRITIONAL ANALYSIS

**EACH WITH:** 135 g water; 254 calories (32% from fat, 14% from protein, 54% from carb); 9 g protein; 10 g total fat; 1 g saturated fat; 2 g monounsaturated fat; 6 g polyunsaturated fat; 36 g carb; 11 g fiber; 12 g sugar; 103 mg calcium; 4 mg iron; 18 mg sodium; 612 mg potassium; 391 IU vitamin A; 9 mg vitamin C; 0 mg cholesterol

# Cucumber and Tomato Pasta Salad

Yield: 8 servings

*A cool and pleasing side dish with a simple dressing.*

2 cups (300 g) pasta

8 ounces (230 g) sour cream

¼ cup (60 ml) skim milk

1 tablespoon (4 g) fresh dill

1 tablespoon (15 ml) vinegar

½ teaspoon black pepper

2 cups (270 g) cucumber, chopped

2 cups (360 g) tomatoes, chopped

Cook pasta in boiling water until al dente. Drain, and rinse in cold water. Transfer cooked pasta to a large serving bowl. In a separate bowl, mix together sour cream, milk, dill, vinegar, and pepper. Set dressing aside. Mix cucumber and tomatoes into the pasta. Pour in dressing and toss thoroughly to combine. Cover and refrigerate for at least 1 hour, preferably overnight. Stir just before serving.

## NUTRITIONAL ANALYSIS

**EACH WITH:** 90 g water; 111 calories (51% from fat, 11% from protein, 38% from carb); 3 g protein; 6 g total fat; 4 g saturated fat; 2 g monounsaturated fat; 0 g polyunsaturated fat; 11 g carb; 1 g fiber; 2 g sugar; 56 mg calcium; 0 mg iron; 24 mg sodium; 208 mg potassium; 549 IU vitamin A; 6 mg vitamin C; 22 mg cholesterol

# Italian Pasta Salad

Yield: 8 servings

*I was looking for something a little different in a cold meal and came up with this. All you need to add is a burger or chicken breast marinated in Italian dressing to make a complete meal.*

1 pound (455 g) elbow macaroni or other shaped pasta

1 pound (455 g) frozen mixed Italian vegetables

½ cup (115 g) low sodium mayonnaise

2 tablespoons (28 ml) olive oil

¼ cup (60 ml) vinegar

1 tablespoon (15 g) Dijon mustard

¼ teaspoon garlic powder

¼ teaspoon onion powder

½ teaspoon sugar

½ teaspoon dried basil

½ teaspoon dried oregano

½ teaspoon dried rosemary

Cook pasta until done; drain and cool. Cook veggies until just crisp; drain and cool. Whisk together remaining ingredients. Pour over pasta and veggies and stir to coat.

### NUTRITIONAL ANALYSIS

**EACH WITH:** 46 g water; 386 calories (35% from fat, 10% from protein, 55% from carb); 10 g protein; 15 g total fat; 2 g saturated fat; 6 g monounsaturated fat; 6 g polyunsaturated fat; 53 g carb; 4 g fiber; 2 g sugar; 37 mg calcium; 3 mg iron; 46 mg sodium; 257 mg potassium; 151 IU vitamin A; 1 mg vitamin C; 8 mg cholesterol

# Potato Salad

Yield: 6 servings

*Traditional picnic fare. Feel free to vary the veggies to whatever suits you best. If you aren't watching your cholesterol, a hard-boiled egg or two would be a nice addition too.*

6 medium potatoes, cubed

½ cup (115 g) low sodium mayonnaise

¼ cup (60 g) sour cream

2 teaspoons (6 g) dry mustard

1 teaspoon onion powder

2 tablespoons (40 g) honey

½ teaspoon black pepper

¼ cup (30 g) green bell pepper, chopped

¼ cup (25 g) celery, sliced

Boil potatoes until done, but not soft. Rinse in cold water and allow to cool. Mix together mayonnaise, sour cream, and seasonings. Pour over potatoes and stir to coat. Fold in chopped veggies.

### NUTRITIONAL ANALYSIS

**EACH WITH:** 338 g water; 453 calories (34% from fat, 7% from protein, 59% from carb); 8 g protein; 17 g total fat; 4 g saturated fat; 5 g monounsaturated fat; 7 g polyunsaturated fat; 68 g carb; 7 g fiber; 11 g sugar; 69 mg calcium; 3 mg iron; 55 mg sodium; 1805 mg potassium; 2799 IU vitamin A; 78 mg vitamin C; 15 mg cholesterol

# Rice Salad

Yield: 4 servings

*Spiced rice dish that can be served either chilled or warm. The spices give a Middle Eastern or Indian sort of flavor.*

- **1 cup (185 g) rice, long cooking**
- **2 tablespoons (28 g) unsalted butter**
- **½ cup (80 g) chopped onion**
- **½ teaspoon garlic, minced**
- **½ teaspoon ground ginger**
- **½ teaspoon ground cinnamon**
- **1 bay leaf**
- **¼ teaspoon ground coriander**
- **¼ teaspoon ground black pepper**
- **¼ teaspoon turmeric**
- **¼ teaspoon ground cumin**
- **⅛ teaspoon cayenne pepper**
- **¼ cup (41 g) golden raisins**
- **¼ cup (31 g) toasted slivered almonds**
- **½ cup (50 g) garbanzo beans, cooked and drained**
- **½ cup (65 g) no-salt-added frozen peas, thawed**

Place the rice in a colander and rinse under cold running water. Place the rinsed rice in a large bowl and cover with 2 cups of water. Let soak for 30 minutes. Drain and reserve the water for cooking. In a large pot, heat the butter over medium-high heat. Add the onion and cook, stirring, for 3 minutes. Add the garlic and ginger, and cook, stirring, for 45 seconds. Add the cinnamon, bay leaf, coriander, pepper, turmeric, cumin, and cayenne, and cook, stirring, until fragrant, about 45 seconds. Add the rice and cook, stirring, for 2 minutes. Add the reserved soaking liquid and raisins, and bring to a boil. Reduce the heat to low, stir, cover, and simmer until the water is absorbed and the rice is tender, about 20 minutes. Remove from the heat and let sit covered for 15 minutes. Fluff the rice with a fork and transfer to a large bowl. Combine with the almonds, beans, and peas. Serve warm or chilled.

---

**NUTRITIONAL ANALYSIS**

**EACH WITH:** 45 g water; 423 calories (26% from fat, 11% from protein, 64% from carb); 12 g protein; 12 g total fat; 4 g saturated fat; 5 g monounsaturated fat; 2 g polyunsaturated fat; 68 g carb; 8 g fiber; 11 g sugar; 100 mg calcium; 4 mg iron; 26 mg sodium; 482 mg potassium; 642 IU vitamin A; 5 mg vitamin C; 15 mg cholesterol

# Couscous Salad

Yield: 6 servings

*For those not familiar with it, couscous is a small pasta popular in Greece, the Middle East, and North Africa. In your favorite health or gourmet food store, you will probably find flavored varieties without salt, but make sure you read the label—the ones found in most grocery stores do contain salt.*

1 cup (175 g) couscous

½ cup (90 g) tomato, coarsely chopped

¼ cup (40 g) green onion, minced

¼ cup (30 g) green bell pepper, coarsely chopped

¼ cup (15 g) fresh parsley, minced

4 tablespoons (60 ml) lemon juice

2½ tablespoons (35 ml) olive oil

1 teaspoon dried oregano

¼ teaspoon black pepper

Cook couscous according to package directions. Transfer the couscous to a bowl and cool. When cool, break apart with a fork. Add the tomato, green onion, bell pepper, and parsley to the couscous. Put the lemon juice, olive oil, oregano, and black pepper into a small jar. Cover and shake well to blend. Pour over the salad, mixing well.

### NUTRITIONAL ANALYSIS

**EACH WITH:** 32 g water; 166 calories (32% from fat, 10% from protein, 59% from carb); 4 g protein; 6 g total fat; 1 g saturated fat; 4 g monounsaturated fat; 1 g polyunsaturated fat; 24 g carb; 2 g fiber; 1 g sugar; 19 mg calcium; 1 mg iron; 6 mg sodium; 125 mg potassium; 381 IU vitamin A; 13 mg vitamin C; 0 mg cholesterol

# Broccoli Salad

Yield: 4 servings

*We've used several different dressings with this salad. It works very well with a cole-slaw-type dressing, but ranch is good too.*

1 cup (70 g) broccoli florets

¼ cup (40 g) red onion, chopped

½ cup (50 g) kidney beans, unsalted

¼ cup (56 g) sunflower seeds, unsalted

Combine ingredients. Add dressing and mix.

### NUTRITIONAL ANALYSIS

**EACH WITH:** 40 g water; 83 calories (41% from fat, 19% from protein, 40% from carb); 4 g protein; 4 g total fat; 0 g saturated fat; 1 g monounsaturated fat; 3 g polyunsaturated fat; 9 g carb; 3 g fiber; 1 g sugar; 31 mg calcium; 1 mg iron; 6 mg sodium; 233 mg potassium; 535 IU vitamin A; 18 mg vitamin C; 0 mg cholesterol

# CHAPTER 12

# Potatoes and Rice

*When I first started the low sodium diet, most of the starchy side dishes we ate were very plain. It was usually baked or boiled potatoes, plain rice, or plain pasta. What could be more boring? But over time I've found a number of ways to add flavor and interest to these kinds of dishes, and that is what this chapter contains.*

# Better Mashed Potatoes

Yield: 4 servings

*This will liven up the flavor of instant mashed potatoes, which tend to be a bit bland when you make them without salt.*

1½ cups (355 ml) low sodium chicken broth

½ cup (120 ml) skim milk

2 tablespoons (28 g) unsalted butter

½ teaspoon onion powder

¼ teaspoon garlic powder

1½ cups (96 g) instant mashed potatoes

Combine all ingredients except potatoes in a saucepan. Bring to boiling. Remove from heat and stir in potatoes. Let stand 5 minutes. Fluff before serving.

## NUTRITIONAL ANALYSIS

**EACH WITH:** 118 g water; 135 calories (39% from fat, 12% from protein, 50% from carb); 4 g protein; 6 g total fat; 4 g saturated fat; 2 g monounsaturated fat; 0 g polyunsaturated fat; 17 g carb; 1 g fiber; 1 g sugar; 59 mg calcium; 0 mg iron; 74 mg sodium; 334 mg potassium; 242 IU vitamin A; 16 mg vitamin C; 16 mg cholesterol

## TIP

Be careful to check the label of the potatoes; some have significant amounts of sodium, particularly the "complete" mixes where you only add water.

# Roasted Garlic Mashed Potatoes

Yield: 4 servings

*These make a flavorful addition to any meal, spicing up a piece of plain grilled meat.*

4 red potatoes

½ teaspoon Roasted Garlic (see recipe, page 32)

2 tablespoons (28 g) unsalted butter

¼ cup (60 ml) skim milk

2 tablespoons (30 g) cream cheese

1 teaspoon dried chives

1 tablespoon (4 g) fresh parsley

Cube the potatoes (you may peel them or leave unpeeled). Place in a saucepan of water, bring to a boil, and simmer until they are soft but not mushy. Drain very well. Place potatoes in a large mixing bowl; add garlic, butter, milk, and cream cheese. Beat until desired consistency, adding more milk if needed, then add the chives and parsley and mix well.

## NUTRITIONAL ANALYSIS

**EACH WITH:** 48 g water; 198 calories (37% from fat, 7% from protein, 55% from carb); 4 g protein; 8 g total fat; 5 g saturated fat; 2 g monounsaturated fat; 0 g polyunsaturated fat; 28 g carb; 5 g fiber; 1 g sugar; 51 mg calcium; 4 mg iron; 44 mg sodium; 378 mg potassium; 402 IU vitamin A; 10 mg vitamin C; 24 mg cholesterol

# Home-Fried Potatoes

Yield: 4 servings

*This is a traditional breakfast kind of dish but also works just as well as a side dish at dinner. Interestingly, the ingredients are almost the same as the latkes, but the flavor is quite different.*

- 4 potatoes
- 1 onion
- 4 tablespoons (55 g) unsalted butter
- ½ teaspoon black pepper

Boil potatoes until almost done. Drain. Coarsely chop potatoes and onion. Melt butter in a heavy skillet. Add potatoes and onion. Grind pepper over. Fry until browned, turning frequently.

## NUTRITIONAL ANALYSIS

**EACH WITH:** 262 g water; 373 calories (28% from fat, 6% from protein, 66% from carb); 6 g protein; 12 g total fat; 7 g saturated fat; 3 g monounsaturated fat; 1 g polyunsaturated fat; 63 g carb; 6 g fiber; 4 g sugar; 35 mg calcium; 1 mg iron; 18 mg sodium; 1033 mg potassium; 365 IU vitamin A; 24 mg vitamin C; 31 mg cholesterol

## TIP

You can also cook the potatoes in the microwave until almost done.

# Hash Browns

Yield: 4 servings

*These are similar to the hash browns served at restaurants. The trick is the soaking in cold water to remove the excess starch. The only problem with that is it tends to make this difficult to do when you just want a quick breakfast.*

- 4 potatoes, shredded
- 2 tablespoons (28 ml) vegetable oil
- ½ teaspoon black pepper
- 1 teaspoon onion powder

Place shredded potatoes in a bowl. Cover with cold water. Add a handful of ice cubes. Place in the refrigerator for 2 hours. Drain and rinse. Heat oil in a heavy skillet. Add potatoes and spread to an even layer. Grind black pepper and sprinkle onion powder on top. Cook until bottom is brown and crisp, 5 to 7 minutes. Turn and cook until other side crisps, about another 5 minutes. Do not stir during cooking.

## NUTRITIONAL ANALYSIS

**EACH WITH:** 232 g water; 321 calories (20% from fat, 6% from protein, 74% from carb); 5 g protein; 7 g total fat; 1 g saturated fat; 2 g monounsaturated fat; 4 g polyunsaturated fat; 61 g carb; 5 g fiber; 3 g sugar; 27 mg calcium; 1 mg iron; 15 mg sodium; 991 mg potassium; 10 IU vitamin A; 22 mg vitamin C; 0 mg cholesterol

# Latkes

Yield: 4 servings

*I'm not Jewish, and I have to admit to having only a basic understanding of kosher food requirements. But this recipe was developed from one on a Jewish food site, so I'm guessing it's a pretty authentic representation of at least one person's idea of what a latke should be like. The squeezing out of the liquid appears to be the critical step in getting a firmly textured patty that will hold together.*

4 potatoes

1 onion

1 tablespoon (8 g) all-purpose flour

1 egg, beaten

½ teaspoon white pepper

2 tablespoons (28 ml) vegetable oil

Peel potatoes. Grate potatoes and onion. Place in a kitchen towel and squeeze out the excess moisture. Combine potato-onion mixture, flour, egg, and pepper. Heat oil in a large skillet. Drop potato-onion mixture into oil with a large tablespoon, using the back of the spoon to spread to an even thickness. Fry until golden brown, about 5 minutes. Turn and fry on the other side until done, about 5 minutes more. Drain on paper towels.

**NUTRITIONAL ANALYSIS**

**EACH WITH:** 270 g water; 360 calories (21% from fat, 8% from protein, 71% from carb); 7 g protein; 9 g total fat; 1 g saturated fat; 2 g monounsaturated fat; 4 g polyunsaturated fat; 65 g carb; 6 g fiber; 4 g sugar; 39 mg calcium; 1 mg iron; 36 mg sodium; 1048 mg potassium; 80 IU vitamin A; 24 mg vitamin C; 61 mg cholesterol

# Potato Dumplings

Yield: 6 servings

*A typical German side dish. Try these with sauerbraten or just plain grilled pork chops.*

6 medium potatoes

1 egg, beaten

3 tablespoons (24 g) cornstarch

1 cup (115 g) low sodium bread crumbs

¼ teaspoon black pepper

¼ cup (28 g) all-purpose flour

Peel potatoes and boil until soft. Drain and mash smoothly. Blend in egg, cornstarch, bread crumbs, and pepper. Mix thoroughly and shape into dumplings, about 1-inch (2.5-cm) balls. You may need to add additional flour to make dumplings hold together. Roll each dumpling in flour and drop into rapidly boiling water. Cover and cook for 15 to 20 minutes.

**NUTRITIONAL ANALYSIS**

**EACH WITH:** 242 g water; 377 calories (5% from fat, 10% from protein, 85% from carb); 9 g protein; 2 g total fat; 1 g saturated fat; 1 g monounsaturated fat; 1 g polyunsaturated fat; 81 g carb; 6 g fiber; 4 g sugar; 63 mg calcium; 2 mg iron; 36 mg sodium; 1038 mg potassium; 56 IU vitamin A; 22 mg vitamin C; 41 mg cholesterol

# Sautéed Garlic Potatoes

Yield: 4 servings

*A nice flavorful side dish to use with a simple grilled piece of meat.*

4 medium red potatoes
1 cup (235 ml) low sodium chicken broth
1 tablespoon (15 ml) olive oil
2 cloves garlic, crushed

Wash potatoes and cut into ½-inch (1¼-cm) cubes; do not peel. Heat chicken broth in a non-stick skillet just large enough to hold the potatoes in 1 layer. Add potatoes, cover, and simmer for 5 minutes. Chicken broth will evaporate during cooking. Add olive oil and garlic. Toss for 5 minutes over medium heat.

### NUTRITIONAL ANALYSIS

**EACH WITH:** 87 g water; 151 calories (20% from fat, 9% from protein, 71% from carb); 3 g protein; 3 g total fat; 0 g saturated fat; 2 g monounsaturated fat; 0 g polyunsaturated fat; 27 g carb; 5 g fiber; 1 g sugar; 27 mg calcium; 4 mg iron; 36 mg sodium; 389 mg potassium; 6 IU vitamin A; 9 mg vitamin C; 0 mg cholesterol

# Potatoes in Spicy Yogurt Sauce

Yield: 6 servings

*These would make a nice alternative to rice for an Indian meal.*

6 medium potatoes, cubed
4 tablespoons (60 ml) olive oil, divided
1 onion, chopped
¼ teaspoon garlic powder
¼ teaspoon ground ginger
½ teaspoon turmeric
2 teaspoons (4 g) coriander
1 teaspoon cumin
¼ teaspoon cardamom
¼ teaspoon chili powder
1 cup (180 g) tomatoes, chopped
1 cup (230 g) plain low-fat yogurt

Preheat oven to 350°F (180°C, gas mark 4). Toss potatoes with 2 tablespoons oil. Bake about 45 minutes, or until potatoes become browned and crisp. Set aside. Heat remaining 2 tablespoons oil in a large, nonstick saucepan and sauté onion until golden. Add garlic powder, ginger, and turmeric. Sauté for 2 minutes. Add remaining spices and tomatoes and sauté for 5 minutes. Stir in the yogurt and the potatoes and simmer gently, covered, for about 30 minutes over low heat, until sauce is thick enough to coat the potatoes.

### NUTRITIONAL ANALYSIS

**EACH WITH:** 308 g water; 340 calories (15% from fat, 9% from protein, 76% from carb); 8 g protein; 6 g total fat; 1 g saturated fat; 4 g monounsaturated fat; 1 g polyunsaturated fat; 66 g carb; 6 g fiber; 7 g sugar; 112 mg calcium; 2 mg iron; 47 mg sodium; 1191 mg potassium; 284 IU vitamin A; 28 mg vitamin C; 2 mg cholesterol

# Yellow Rice

Yield: 6 servings

*This is similar to the Spanish-style saffron rice, only without the sodium or the saffron. The turmeric gives it a nice yellow color at a lot cheaper price than saffron and doesn't really affect the flavor.*

2 tablespoons (28 ml) olive oil

½ cup (80 g) onion, chopped

¼ cup (30 g) red bell pepper, finely chopped

¼ cup (30 g) green bell pepper, finely chopped

1 cup (195 g) uncooked rice

½ cup (75 g) orzo or other small pasta

3¼ cups (765 ml) water

¼ teaspoon black pepper

1 teaspoon cumin

1 teaspoon onion powder

½ teaspoon garlic powder

½ teaspoon turmeric

Sauté onion and peppers in oil until tender. Add rice and orzo or pasta and sauté about 2 minutes longer or until pasta is golden brown. Add water and spices, cover, reduce heat, and simmer for 20 minutes or until rice is tender.

### NUTRITIONAL ANALYSIS

**EACH WITH:** 150 g water; 198 calories (23% from fat, 7% from protein, 70% from carb); 4 g protein; 5 g total fat; 1 g saturated fat; 3 g monounsaturated fat; 1 g polyunsaturated fat; 34 g carb; 1 g fiber; 1 g sugar; 32 mg calcium; 2 mg iron; 6 mg sodium; 100 mg potassium; 112 IU vitamin A; 9 mg vitamin C; 0 mg cholesterol

# Brown Rice Pilaf

Yield: 4 servings

*When I make something like this it makes me wonder why I don't cook brown rice more often. It has such a nice flavor and crunchy texture.*

2 cups (475 ml) low sodium chicken broth

½ cup (120 ml) water

1 cup (190 g) uncooked brown rice

2 tablespoons (20 g) onion, minced

⅛ teaspoon garlic powder

Place broth and water in a saucepan. Bring to a boil. Add the rice and the spices. Reduce heat, cover, and simmer for 30 minutes or until rice is done.

### NUTRITIONAL ANALYSIS

**EACH WITH:** 156 g water; 182 calories (7% from fat, 12% from protein, 81% from carb); 5 g protein; 1 g total fat; 0 g saturated fat; 0 g monounsaturated fat; 0 g polyunsaturated fat; 37 g carb; 2 g fiber; 1 g sugar; 22 mg calcium; 1 mg iron; 52 mg sodium; 213 mg potassium; 0 IU vitamin A; 1 mg vitamin C; 0 mg cholesterol

# Italian Rice

Yield: 6 servings

*I guess I just get bored easily, but I'm always looking for a way to make things a little different. Don't get me wrong—I love plain rice. I could make a meal on a nice bowlful fresh out of the steamer with nothing on it at all. But somehow that seems too plain for a meal. So we added a few Italian things to give you a different side dish. I served it with a grilled piece of fish that had been marinated in Italian dressing.*

¼ cup (40 g) onion, chopped

2 tablespoons (28 ml) olive oil

1 cup (195 g) uncooked rice

2¼ cups (535 ml) water

¼ teaspoon garlic powder

¼ cup (14 g) sun-dried tomatoes, chopped

Sauté onion in olive oil in a heavy saucepan. Add rice and continue cooking until it begins to brown. Add water and other ingredients. Cover and simmer for 20 minutes or until the rice is tender.

NUTRITIONAL ANALYSIS

**EACH WITH:** 118 g water; 86 calories (54% from fat, 5% from protein, 41% from carb); 1 g protein; 5 g total fat; 1 g saturated fat; 4 g monounsaturated fat; 1 g polyunsaturated fat; 9 g carb; 0 g fiber; 0 g sugar; 11 mg calcium; 0 mg iron; 15 mg sodium; 93 mg potassium; 59 IU vitamin A; 5 mg vitamin C; 0 mg cholesterol

# Lemon-Herb Rice

Yield: 4 servings

*This was just a quick stir-together side dish to serve with fish. You could add additional herbs depending on the meal and your tastes. It's also a good way to use leftover rice.*

2 cups (330 g) rice, cooked

¼ cup (60 ml) low sodium chicken broth

2 tablespoons (28 ml) lemon juice

¼ teaspoon garlic powder

½ teaspoon onion powder

1 tablespoon (0.4 g) dried parsley

¼ teaspoon black pepper

Stir all ingredients together in a saucepan or microwave-safe bowl and heat through.

NUTRITIONAL ANALYSIS

**EACH WITH:** 86 g water; 105 calories (2% from fat, 9% from protein, 89% from carb); 2 g protein; 0 g total fat; 0 g saturated fat; 0 g monounsaturated fat; 0 g polyunsaturated fat; 23 g carb; 0 g fiber; 0 g sugar; 21 mg calcium; 1 mg iron; 9 mg sodium; 66 mg potassium; 81 IU vitamin A; 5 mg vitamin C; 0 mg cholesterol

# Mushroom Rice

Yield: 6 servings

*Just like the ones that come in the packaged mixes and almost as easy to cook. Plus you are allowed to eat this lower-sodium version.*

8 ounces (225 g) mushrooms, sliced

2 tablespoons (28 g) unsalted butter

¼ teaspoon garlic powder

1 tablespoon (10 g) minced onion

1 tablespoon (0.4 g) dried parsley

1½ cups (292 g) uncooked rice

2 cups (475 ml) low sodium chicken broth

1⅓ cups (315 ml) water

¼ cup (28 g) nonfat dry milk powder

In a large skillet, sauté the mushrooms in the butter until brown. Add the spices and rice and continue cooking until the rice begins to brown, stirring occasionally. Add the chicken broth and water, cover, and return to boil. Lower heat and simmer until rice is tender and liquid absorbed, about 20 minutes. Stir in the milk powder.

### NUTRITIONAL ANALYSIS

**EACH WITH:** 199 g water; 111 calories (33% from fat, 16% from protein, 52% from carb); 4 g protein; 4 g total fat; 2 g saturated fat; 1 g monounsaturated fat; 0 g polyunsaturated fat; 15 g carb; 1 g fiber; 3 g sugar; 56 mg calcium; 1 mg iron; 52 mg sodium; 271 mg potassium; 238 IU vitamin A; 3 mg vitamin C; 11 mg cholesterol

# Mexican Rice

Yield: 4 servings

*A simple-to-make and flavorful Mexican side dish. If you fill up on this you'll be less likely to eat as much of the other higher-fat and higher-sodium things.*

1 cup (195 g) uncooked rice

⅓ cup (55 g) onion, chopped

⅓ cup (40 g) green bell pepper, chopped

2 cups (475 ml) no-salt-added tomatoes

2 tablespoons (28 ml) vegetable oil

¼ tablespoon black pepper

1 teaspoon Worcestershire sauce

1 teaspoon low sodium beef bouillon

1 cup (235 ml) water

Sauté rice, onion, and bell pepper in oil in a heavy saucepan until onion is tender. Add the remaining ingredients and bring to a boil. Reduce heat, cover, and simmer until rice is tender, about 20 minutes.

### NUTRITIONAL ANALYSIS

**EACH WITH:** 221 g water; 142 calories (44% from fat, 6% from protein, 50% from carb); 2 g protein; 7 g total fat; 1 g saturated fat; 2 g monounsaturated fat; 4 g polyunsaturated fat; 18 g carb; 2 g fiber; 4 g sugar; 50 mg calcium; 1 mg iron; 41 mg sodium; 336 mg potassium; 195 IU vitamin A; 25 mg vitamin C; 0 mg cholesterol

# Fried Rice

Yield: 6 servings

*This is similar to the fried rice flavor of Rice-a-Roni. I don't know if any of you have been missing that kind of boxed convenience or not, but this is very nearly as easy to make (just a little extra measuring) and a whole lot better for you.*

- 1 cup (185 g) long grain rice
- ½ cup (75 g) orzo or other small pasta
- 2 tablespoons (28 ml) vegetable oil
- 3½ cups (825 ml) water
- ½ teaspoon onion powder
- ¼ teaspoon garlic powder
- 1 teaspoon dried parsley
- 1 tablespoon (7 g) Asian Seasoning (see recipe, page 16)
- ¼ cup (60 ml) Soy Sauce Substitute (see recipe, page 28)

Sauté rice and pasta in oil about for 2 minutes or until pasta is golden brown. Add water, spices, and soy sauce substitute. Cover, reduce heat, and simmer for 20 minutes or until rice is tender.

### NUTRITIONAL ANALYSIS

**EACH WITH:** 143 g water; 186 calories (24% from fat, 7% from protein, 69% from carb); 3 g protein; 5 g total fat; 1 g saturated fat; 1 g monounsaturated fat; 3 g polyunsaturated fat; 31 g carb; 1 g fiber; 0 g sugar; 14 mg calcium; 2 mg iron; 5 mg sodium; 54 mg potassium; 18 IU vitamin A; 0 mg vitamin C; 0 mg cholesterol

# Confetti Couscous

Yield: 4 servings

*For anyone not familiar with couscous, it's a very small Middle Eastern pasta. It can be used as a base for curries, tomato-based sauces, or any number of other things or by itself as a side dish. This variation adds a few veggies for flavor and color.*

- ¼ cup (40 g) onion, finely chopped
- ¼ cup (30 g) red bell pepper, finely chopped
- ¼ cup (30 g) celery, finely chopped
- 1 tablespoon (15 ml) olive oil
- 1½ cups (355 ml) low sodium chicken broth
- 1 cup (175 g) couscous

Sauté veggies in oil until tender. Bring broth to a boil. Stir in couscous and veggies. Cover and let stand for 5 minutes. Fluff with a fork before serving.

### NUTRITIONAL ANALYSIS

**EACH WITH:** 112 g water; 205 calories (16% from fat, 14% from protein, 70% from carb); 7 g protein; 4 g total fat; 1 g saturated fat; 3 g monounsaturated fat; 0 g polyunsaturated fat; 35 g carb; 3 g fiber; 1 g sugar; 23 mg calcium; 1 mg iron; 46 mg sodium; 192 mg potassium; 178 IU vitamin A; 10 mg vitamin C; 0 mg cholesterol

# About the Author

*Dick Logue had a low sodium lifestyle forced upon him when he was diagnosed with congestive heart failure. He decided to use his love of cooking to help him create low sodium versions of the foods he loved. He lives on a little farm in the woods of southern Maryland with his wife Ginger, two of their three children, and an assortment of animals.*

# INDEX